Timesaver Customs & Lifestyle in the UK & Ireland

(Pre-Intermediate – Upper-Intermediate)

Julia Starr Keddle
and Martyn Hobbs

■ SCHOLASTIC

MARY GLASGOW MAGAZINES

Introduction

Timesaver Customs & Lifestyle in the UK & Ireland presents aspects of British and Irish culture and lifestyle from a teenage perspective. Each lesson is centred around a variety of topics from geography and history to day-to-day teenage life in multicultural Britain. The materials provide English language learners with stimulating activities for discussion and comparison with their own cultures and experiences. They also provide the teacher with interesting and rewarding lessons that involve minimal preparation.

ABOUT THIS BOOK

This book is divided into fourteen topics. The topics are outlined below and listed on the Contents page (pages 4–5). Within each topic there are three varied lessons at three different levels.

 pre-intermediate – for students with 1–2 years of English.

 intermediate – for students with 2–3 years of English.

 upper-intermediate – for students with more than 3 years of English.

Each lesson consists of a double page of activities. The three lessons within a topic each cover a different aspect of the topic, so you can use more than one lesson with higher level classes and they will still find the material stimulating and interesting. The length of the lessons will vary depending on the level of the class and how the activities are tackled. Activities can be exploited in different ways according to their appropriacy for the students in your class.

Most of the lessons contain presentation material, which introduces the topic and gives the students information about the subject. This is followed by activities that help the students understand the text, including matching, true/false activities, gap filling, quizzes, scanning and skimming activities. The second page usually provides extension of the topic and/or consolidation activities in the form of games and puzzles. Photocopy both pages of your chosen lesson for each student so that the lesson progresses from presentation to freer activities.

The types of activity are varied and include individual, pairwork and groupwork activities, plus activities that can be used for homework. Some of the activities are open-ended or lead on to discussion and extension work; others have specific answers. There is an answer key at the back of this book. Refer to this to check students' work as a whole class, or photocopy it and distribute it for individual or pair checking.

Many of the topics lead naturally on to further project work. Students can prepare projects based on British and Irish culture or based on aspects of their own culture. The websites below provide more information on the topics in this book.

VOCABULARY

Vocabulary is graded according to topic and level. The language used is natural and appropriate to the topic and the age group. Some topics require more advanced vocabulary and students at all levels will find dictionaries or teacher input useful. You will notice that some of the words or phrases in each lesson have an asterisk (*). These are words that might be beyond the level of the students, that are not illustrated or explained on the page and that students may not be able to guess from context. The note *What is it in your language? Find out!* invites the students to use their dictionaries and is an opportunity for them to improve their study skills. Alternatively, the teacher can pre-teach the words, or (in a monolingual classroom) provide translations.

TOPICS

What is Britain?

This unit is a lively introduction to the geography and history of England, Wales, Scotland, Ireland and Northern Ireland. There is a lot of material on the Internet about Britain, especially in relation to tourism.

Useful web addresses:
- www.number-10.gov.uk **(UK)**
- www.tourist-information-uk.com **(UK)**
- www.visitbritain.com **(UK)**
- www.geo.ed.ac.uk/home/scotland/touristinfo.html **(Scotland)**
- www.ireland.ie **(Ireland)**

Culture and the city

This unit presents three fashionable cities in the UK and Ireland. Dublin, the capital of Ireland, is a lively city full of young professional people and tourists. Brighton is a seaside resort famous for its vibrant atmosphere, and Liverpool was an industrial port that has transformed itself into an attractive tourist venue.

Useful web addresses:
- www.visitdublin.com **(Dublin)**
- www.tourist-information-dublin.co.uk **(Dublin)**
- www.visitbrighton.com **(Brighton)**
- www.visitliverpool.com **(Liverpool)**
- www.merseyworld.com/tourism/attractions **(Liverpool)**

Multicultural Britain

This unit introduces students to Britain as a multicultural country through the experiences of British teenagers. It gives students information about the ethnic groups that live in Britain through a variety of texts including students talking about their families, an introduction to teenage slang, fact files and articles about new multicultural influences.

Useful web addresses:
- www.movinghere.org.uk **(life in the UK)**
- www.cre.gov.uk/ethdiv/ethdiv.html **(multicultural facts)**
- www.britkid.org **(interactive teenage site)**
- www.bbc.co.uk/schools/gcsebitesize/music/worldmusic **(world music)**

Sport

The British and Irish are sporting nations and this unit provides information about some favourite sports – football, cricket and rugby.

Useful web addresses:
- www.britishsports.com **(sport)**
- www.campaigns.visitbritain.com/uktheguide/uk/sporting/uk **(sport)**
- www.footballculture.net **(football)**
- www.cs.purdue.edu/homes/hosking/cricket **(cricket)**

Music and fashion

This unit gives students an interesting and interactive history of pop music and fashion from a British perspective. Students are shown the contribution made by British musicians to the development of pop and rock and they see the links between fashion and music over the past fifty years.

Useful web addresses:
- www.home.clara.net/digger/sixties/events **(1960s)**
- www.fashion-era.com/1970s.htm **(1970s)**

British waters

The UK and Ireland are surrounded by water and people enjoy going to the seaside and having fun on rivers. This unit gives students an insight into the British at the beach on holiday and British people who live in cities near water.

Useful web addresses:
- www.riverthames.co.uk **(The Thames)**
- www.liverpoolcanallink.co.uk/merseyfest.htm **(Liverpool)**
- www.thisisoxfordshire.co.uk/oxfordshire/visit/attractions **(Oxford)**
- www.stratford-upon-avon.co.uk **(Stratford-upon-Avon)**
- www.seeglasgow.com **(Glasgow)**
- www.blackpooltourism.com **(Blackpool)**
- www.bournemouth.co.uk **(Bournemouth)**
- www.newquay.co.uk **(Newquay)**
- www.wales-calling.com/guide/brecon.htm **(Wales)**
- www.visithighlands.com/northern-scottish-highlands **(Scotland)**

Going out

The British love going out and this unit presents the opportunities teenagers have from going to the cinema and having a pizza, to days out at theme parks. It also includes information about pubs – not a venue for teenagers but an essential part of the British and Irish street scene and lifestyle.

Useful web addresses:
- www.paultonspark.co.uk **(Paultons Park)**
- www.ryedalefolkmuseum.co.uk **(Rydale Folk Museum)**
- www.bbc.co.uk/gloucestershire/sport/extreme_sports/paintballing.shtml **(paintballing)**
- www.historic-uk.com/CultureUK/Pubsigns.htm **(pubs)**

Festivals and fun

Summer fetes, carnivals, music and theatre, festivals and dancing – these are all different ways in which British and Irish people have fun. Students learn about a variety of typical aspects of these activities.

Useful web addresses:
- www.overvillage.co.uk/carnival2004.htm **(carnival))**
- www.bbc.co.uk/dna/h2g2/A358788 **(fete)**
- www.glastonburyfestivals.co.uk **(Glastonbury festival)**
- www.eif.co.uk **(Edinburgh Festival)**
- womad.org **(WOMAD)**
- www.reading-festival.org.uk **(Reading festival)**
- www.edinburghtango.org.uk/latin/salsa_music_guide.html **(salsa)**
- www.communigate.co.uk/york/gravitycontrolcrew/index.phtml **(breakdancing)**
- www.cam.ac.uk/societies/round/ceilidh.htm **(ceilidh)**

Shopping

Every teenager loves shopping and this unit explores the things that British teenagers spend their money on.

Useful web addresses:
• www.bbc.co.uk/coventry/features/teens/stories/teens-coventry-shopping.shtml **(clothes shopping)**
• www.oxfam.org.uk/what_you_can_do/shop **(charity shops)**

World of work

Although their parents pay for the essentials, teenagers in the UK and Ireland earn pocket money at home and do a lot of part time jobs to get extra money. This gives them both independence and a sense of responsibility. This unit explores the different jobs teenagers do.

Useful web addresses:
• www.tiscali.co.uk/money/features/pocketmoney/2 **(pocket money)**
• www.work-experience.org/cms **(work experience)**

Schools

This unit explores students' experience of school. It looks at school rules in the UK, school subjects, the education system, and one student's diary of a day at school.

Useful web addresses:
• www.justdosomething.net/xsp/xsc.asp?uri=/home/zone/uk-guide/education-s/the-different-stages-of-school **(school)**
• www.bbc.co.uk/schools **(school)**

Food and drink

Food and drink tell us a lot about people and their lifestyles. In this unit, we explore typical teenage breakfasts and lunches, comfort food and the ever-popular ethnic favourites, not forgetting Britain's favourite drink – tea.

Useful web addresses:
• www.oxfam.org.uk/coolplanet/ontheline/explore/journey/uk/food.htm **(food)**
• www.bbc.co.uk/food/recipes/mostof_tea.shtml **(tea)**

The British home and lifestyle

People in the UK and Ireland love their homes. But what are they like? This unit explores typical British homes, their rooms and furniture and customs in the home.

Useful web addresses:
• www.ukstudentlife.com/Personal/Manners.htm **(customs)**
• www.bbc.co.uk/homes **(homes and lifestyle)**

Celebrations

The British and Irish like to have a party or celebrate a special day. This unit talks about greetings cards, special days, school proms and fireworks.

Useful web addresses:
• www.birthdays.co.uk/whatsnew/history_main.htm **(cards)**
• www.perfectproms.com **(Proms)**
• www.fireworks.co.uk/heritage/history.html **(fireworks)**

All website addresses were correct at time of publication. Mary Glasgow Magazines is not responsible for any changes to content on the websites listed here.

Contents

England

When you hear the word 'England', you probably think of red buses, pretty villages* and postcards of Buckingham Palace. But did you know about the music festival* in Glastonbury, the great fashion and music in London and the best night life in Europe in Birmingham? Read some facts about England and look at the map.

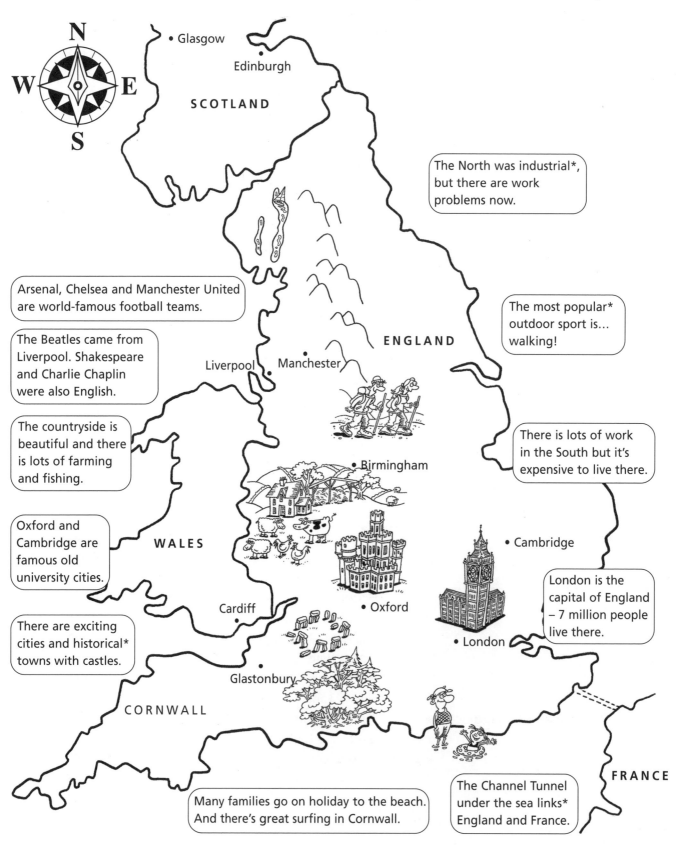

The North was industrial*, but there are work problems now.

Arsenal, Chelsea and Manchester United are world-famous football teams.

The Beatles came from Liverpool. Shakespeare and Charlie Chaplin were also English.

The most popular* outdoor sport is… walking!

The countryside is beautiful and there is lots of farming and fishing.

There is lots of work in the South but it's expensive to live there.

Oxford and Cambridge are famous old university cities.

There are exciting cities and historical* towns with castles.

London is the capital of England – 7 million people live there.

Many families go on holiday to the beach. And there's great surfing in Cornwall.

The Channel Tunnel under the sea links* England and France.

Info-stop

Is England the same as Britain?

- No. England, Scotland and Wales are all countries in Britain. Britain is the largest island in Europe.

Is Britain the same as the UK?

- No. The UK is Britain and Northern Ireland.
- The UK is a member* of the European Union.

Is Queen Elizabeth the Queen of England?

- Yes, and more! She's the Queen of the whole of the UK. She lives in Buckingham Palace in England and she's got a home in Scotland.

What is the Union flag?

- The red St George's Cross of England, the red St Patrick's Cross of Ireland and the white St Andrew's Cross of Scotland on a blue background* make the Union flag.

Look at the key and complete the map.

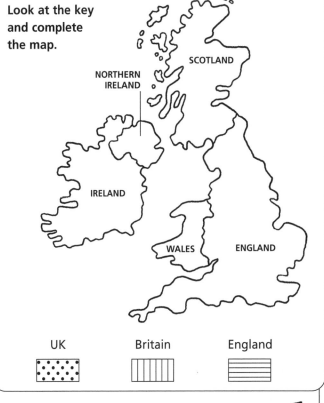

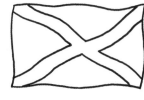

Colour the flags.

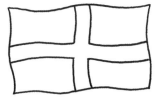

England   Ireland   Scotland   Union flag

Dan is visiting England. Find ten mistakes in his email. Rewrite it with the correct information.

To: Lisa@email.com
Cc: Hello from London
Subject:
Account:

Hi Lisa

Here I am in London. It's the capital of Britain. It's a huge place – ten million people live here. That's crowded*!
The Queen lives in Birmingham Palace.
England is really cool. Cambridge is amazing. It's got the best night life in the world.
The English are so funny. Many people go to the mountains for their holidays. There's great skiing in Cornwall. But did you know? Fishing is their favourite outdoor sport!
Britain is the smallest island in Europe. The Channel Bridge goes from England to Spain.
See you soon
Dan x

* What is it in your language? Find out!

Wales and Scotland
Wales

Info-stop

- This is the Welsh flag – The Red Dragon of Wales.

- The Welsh language is one of the oldest in Europe. 20% of the population* speaks Welsh.

- Do you like vegetables? The Welsh national symbol is a leek.

- Are you good at spelling? A town in Wales has the longest name in Britain! Llanfairpwllgwyngyllgogerychwyrndrobwllllantty-siliogogogoch

- There are lots of castles in Wales. They were built in the Middle Ages*, when the Welsh fought the English.

- Wales is called Cymru in Welsh.

- Don't call Welsh people English. They aren't. They're Welsh!

- Every year there are music and art festivals called Eisteddfods. They began around 1,000 years ago.

Read about Wales. Find the places on the map and write the letters.

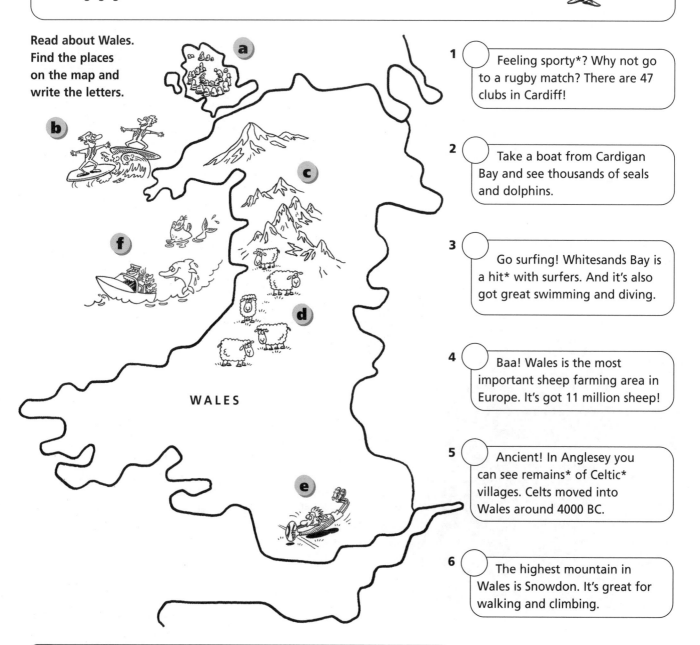

1 Feeling sporty*? Why not go to a rugby match? There are 47 clubs in Cardiff!

2 Take a boat from Cardigan Bay and see thousands of seals and dolphins.

3 Go surfing! Whitesands Bay is a hit* with surfers. And it's also got great swimming and diving.

4 Baa! Wales is the most important sheep farming area in Europe. It's got 11 million sheep!

5 Ancient! In Anglesey you can see remains* of Celtic* villages. Celts moved into Wales around 4000 BC.

6 The highest mountain in Wales is Snowdon. It's great for walking and climbing.

Scotland

Jo is on holiday in Scotland. Complete her emails with the missing verbs in the past tense. Then match them to the pictures.

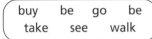

buy   be   go   be
take   see   walk

* What is it in your language?
Find out!

1

To: helen@email.com
Cc: Hello from Scotland
Subject:
Account:

We .... in Glasgow yesterday. I thought it was the capital of Scotland. Wrong! But Glasgow *is* the style capital of Scotland. We .... shopping this morning. Some shops sell Scottish things like Tartan. That's a traditional cloth. My brother said he wanted to buy a kilt (a skirt for men). But he was only joking! He .... a tartan hat instead. ◯

2

To: helen@email.com
Cc: Hello from Scotland
Subject:
Account:

Hi! We're in the North of Scotland now. We're at the Highland games. They do some crazy sports. One of them is called 'tossing the caber' where men throw a heavy wooden pole*! At the weekend we went to Ben Nevis, Britain's highest mountain. We .... to the top. It was really tiring*. ◯

3

To: helen@email.com
Cc: Hello from Scotland
Subject:
Account:

I'm sending this from Loch Ness – the lake with the famous monster. We went out on a boat this morning but we didn't .... the monster! And two days ago we .... a ferry* to the Orkney Islands (Scotland has 800 islands!), and we saw thousands of birds. They were so noisy! ◯

4

To: helen@email.com
Cc: Hello from Scotland
Subject:
Account:

We're having a great time in Edinburgh. That's right, the capital of Scotland! It's really crowded because there's an international arts festival – there are hundreds of shows! We went to one last night – it .... great. And we climbed up to the Castle, too. I saw somebody playing traditional music on bagpipes. ◯

Ireland and Northern Ireland

Info-stop

What is Northern Ireland?
- It's physically* part of the island of Ireland.
- It's politically* part of the UK.

What is Ireland?
- It's a country and a member of the European Union.

What is Eire?
- It's the Gaelic* name for Ireland. You can say Ireland or Eire.

Did you know?
- Don't call Irish people British. They aren't. They're Irish!

Is Queen Elizabeth the Queen of Ireland?
- No, she isn't. She's the Queen of the UK so she's only the Queen of Northern Ireland.

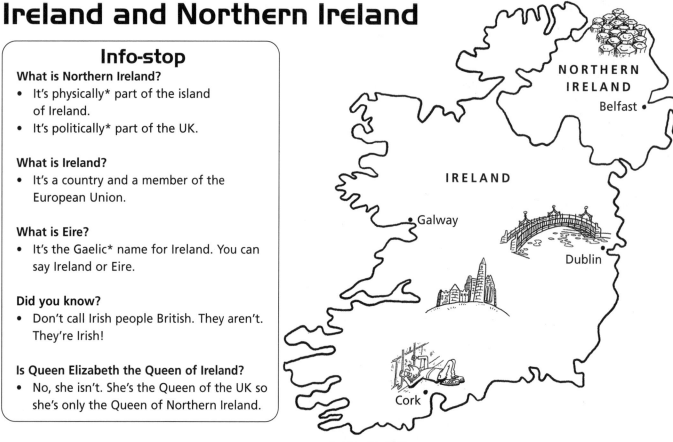

Find someone who ...

1 finds the place where they live boring. ....

2 can speak Gaelic. ....

3 is studying computer technology. ....

4 wants to study in London. ....

5 wants to live abroad. ....

6 is interested in fashion. ....

7 hates folk music. ....

8 lives in a small lively city. ....

9 never wants to leave Ireland. ....

10 plays traditional Irish music. ....

I live in Belfast. It's a modern city. It's had some troubles in the past but now it's a safe place to live. There are lots of clubs for young people and things to do. I like clothes and I'd like to be a fashion designer. Belfast has a good university but I'd like to study in London.
Jonny

I'm a Dubliner and Dublin is the coolest city in Ireland. It's home to U2, the best band in the world, and lots of foreign students come to Trinity College, the university. I never want to leave Dublin. I'm studying computer technology, Nowadays there are lots of job opportunities here.
Cait

I come from Galway on the West coast. It's a small city but very lively. It's full of young people and university students. I play in an Irish folk band and we do gigs* in pubs and bars. I'm really into Celtic mythology and I'm fluent in Gaelic. When I want to get away from the crowds, I cycle down to the sea. I love watching the waves come in.
Liam

I'm from Allihies, a small village in the county of West Cork. It's a bit boring here. There are lots of pubs, but nothing for young people to do. Everyone is into Irish folk music, which I hate! I love dance music. Cork's got a good music scene but it takes hours to get there by bus. I want to go to Dublin and study languages. Then I'd love to live abroad.
Eileen

The Giant's Causeway is an amazing volcanic* rock formation in Northern Ireland. It is made up of hundreds of huge, hexagonal pillars* of stone.
Join up the information to find out more about Ireland.

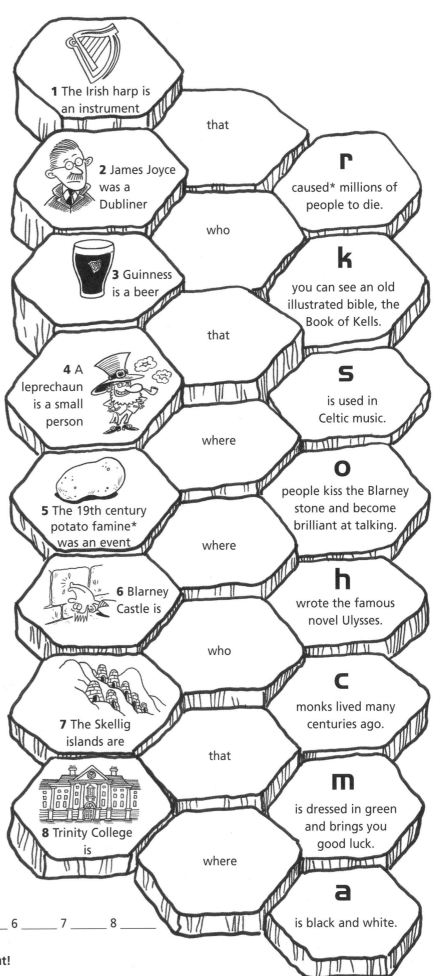

1 The Irish harp is an instrument

that

r caused* millions of people to die.

2 James Joyce was a Dubliner

who

k you can see an old illustrated bible, the Book of Kells.

3 Guinness is a beer

that

s is used in Celtic music.

4 A leprechaun is a small person

where

o people kiss the Blarney stone and become brilliant at talking.

5 The 19th century potato famine* was an event

where

h wrote the famous novel Ulysses.

6 Blarney Castle is

who

c monks lived many centuries ago.

7 The Skellig islands are

that

m is dressed in green and brings you good luck.

8 Trinity College is

where

a is black and white.

Write the letters in order and find the name of a lucky Irish plant.

1 _____ 2 _____ 3 _____ 4 _____ 5 _____ 6 _____ 7 _____ 8 _____

* What is it in your language? Find out!

My Dublin

Info-stop

- Dublin is the capital of Ireland.

- Three million people, or about half of Ireland's population*, live here.

- Dublin has a very young population and it is an exciting place to live.

- It's a great place to visit as there are lots of things to see and over a thousand pubs and clubs. Groups of young friends come from abroad to celebrate their stag[1] and hen[2] nights here.

Great things to do

Read what ten young Dubliners said about their favourite things.
Write the titles in the correct places. Then number the places on the map on the next page.

See how the Vikings lived
Eat out
Go green

Go shopping
Go to college
See how Guinness is made

1 ....

I go shopping in Grafton Street. It's in the city centre, and there are always lots of shoppers and street performers*. I usually just look at the shop windows or meet my friends.
Siobhan

2 ....

There are always lots of students there, but the place to go is Trinity College. It is a very old building in the centre of the city. I love visiting the Book of Kells, an amazing medieval* book. The gift shop is cool too!
Keiran

3 ....

Temple Bar is the coolest place on the planet*! You can eat all kinds of food here. There are lots of cafés and pubs too. After your meal you can walk along the River Liffey.
Clare

4 ....

Guinness, the famous stout (dark beer), is made here. Dublin has the largest stout brewery* in the world and makes 450 million litres a year. The multimedia museum is the most popular place in town.
Hannah

5 ....

Dublin was a Viking city called Dyflin. The Viking Splash Tour is a ride in a truck that goes on water like a boat – mega-cool! And really wet! I like Dublin's Viking Adventure, too. You can visit the streets of 1,000 years ago.
Emma

6 ....

Green is the colour of Ireland and there are lots of green spaces here. Phoenix Park is the biggest park in the world. There's a zoo and a visitors' centre. I love going there for a picnic with my friends.
Laila

Which things would you like to do in Dublin? You can choose three. Discuss your ideas with your partner.

Dublin

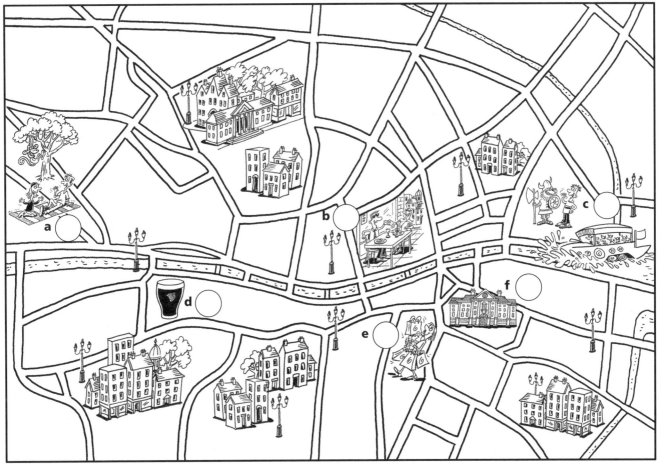

The Claddagh ring

Irish and Celtic mythology* is full of symbols*. This Celtic ring is still worn by people all over the world. It's from an Irish fisherman's village called Claddagh. Find the ring by colouring in the picture. (1 = yellow 2 = red 3 = blue). Then do the anagrams and read about the ring.

The **raeht** .... represents* love.

The **sndah** .... represent friendship.

The **norcw** .... represents fidelity*.

Glossary: [1] stag night – an evening out with male friends for a young man who is going to get married.
[2] hen night – an evening out with female friends for a young woman who is going to get married.

* What is it in your language? Find out!

Brighton rocks!

Info-stop

- Brighton is one of the UK's top ten tourist destinations* with its fashionable shops, colourful houses and seaside promenades*.
- In Victorian times it was called 'London by the sea'.
- On sunny weekends lots of British people go to Brighton for the day. There's lots for all the family to do. Teenagers love the pier* and all the family enjoys the beach and the shopping!

Match the photos to the texts. Then write the numbers in brackets in the correct places on the map on the next page.

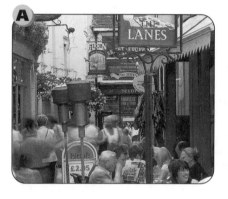

◯ **The Pavilion**

Visit the Brighton Pavilion [1] – built in 1822, it is a fantastic royal, oriental* palace with dragons and golden ceilings.

◯ **The Palace Pier and Sea Life Centre**

Go to the Palace Pier [2]. Don't miss the Pleasure Dome with video games, fairground rides, and karaoke sessions*. Or meet sharks face-to-face at the Sea Life Centre [3].

◯ **The shops**

The North Laines [4] have got lots of small shops where all the cool people hang out*. It's a great place to get unusual clothes. Shopping in The Lanes [5] is fun, too. It was an old fishing village but now it has continental cafés, jewellery, music and gift shops.

◯ **The promenade**

Go to the beach front Promenade [6] and snack on take-away seafood. Or try a really traditional* British dish – fish and chips. If you like sweet food try some Brighton Rock – a traditional candy stick.

◯ **The festival**

In May there is the Brighton festival with fun fairs, street theatre and shows. Film fanatics* can watch a film at the Duke of York's Media Centre [7] – it has 23 screens!

◯ **Sports**

If sport is more your style, cycle along the seafront or go to the King Alfred Leisure Centre [8] and go bowling and swimming. Or stay by the beach and go sailing or windsurfing. You can also do in-line skating* on the promenade.

Plan a day trip to Brighton with your partner. Choose three things to do.

Where are Tim and Suzy? Read the text messages and write the places.

1 I DON'T THINK I LIKE SHARKS VERY MUCH. TOO MANY TEETH!

....

2 I'M LOOKING AT AN AMAZING DRAGON. ....

3 I'M EATING FISH AND CHIPS BY THE SEA. TASTY! ....

4 WE'RE ON A GREAT RIDE BUT IT'S NOT VERY FAST. ....

5 WE'RE BOWLING AND I'M WINNING! ....

6 I DON'T KNOW WHICH FILM TO SEE. ....

7 SUZY'S CHOOSING SOME JEWELLERY FOR HER MUM. ....

Tim and Suzy met two friends at Palace Pier. Which of the prizes below did they win? (Use the code breaker at the bottom of the page if you need help.)

Suzy won .... Tim won .... Anne won .... Adam won ....

Code breaker: 1 s 2 f 3 j 4 o 5 a 6 n 7 l 8 u 9 b 10 v 11 p 12 z 13 14 c
15 y 16 d 17 q 18 w 19 e 20 i 21 g 22 r 23 m 24 h 25 k 26 t

* **What is it in your language? Find out!**

Beatlemania in Liverpool

1 ....

2 ....

David is in Liverpool.
Read his diary and write the days next to the pictures.

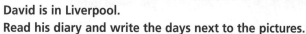

Monday

Liverpool *is* the Beatles. We went to the Beatles Story, all about the Fab Four. They invented* 'cool'. Did you know the Beatles did 275 gigs* between 1961 and 1963? In the afternoon we went on a Magical Mystery* Tour on a bus to see places from the Beatles songs. We saw Strawberry Fields, Penny Lane, and Paul McCartney's childhood* home.

Tuesday

We went to the Museum of Liverpool life. The city is famous for trade, football (Liverpool and Everton) and horse racing. In the afternoon we took a ferry across the River Mersey. We saw the world famous Liver Building. It's got two metal birds on it called the Liver Birds.

Wednesday

Liverpool is a city of docks* and boats. We went to the Merseyside Maritime museum. It had really good models of ships and a history of slavery*. On the top floor was a great café.

Thursday

We took a boat trip from the Pier Head and saw great views of the skyline. Then we saw sharks at the Blue Planet Aquarium – it's got the world's longest walk through an underwater tunnel. It was cool seeing all the sea animals. In the afternoon I took a photo of the Cavern Wall of Fame, which has all the names of artists and bands who played at the Cavern – that's a club.

Friday

Shopping! It's not my scene, really. But Albert Dock is in warehouse* buildings by the docks – I love boats and there are lots of cafés as well as shops there so I was happy. After lunch we had our last trip on the water in the Yellow Duckmarine! Get it? The 'Yellow submarine'! Dad sang the song – how embarrassing*!

Which things would you like to do in Liverpool? You can choose three. Discuss your ideas with your partner.

3 ....

4 ....

5 ....

Use words from the information about Liverpool to do the crossword.

Info-stop

- Liverpool is the European Capital of Culture for 2008.
- It is the most filmed British city outside London!
- It has a population of 450,000.
- It has two cathedrals* and lots of museums and tourist sights.
- It has a busy and active* port.
- It is the home of the Beatles. And it's still the city of pop – many successful new bands come from Liverpool.

Across

1 a large church
3 the Beatles were known as the fab _____ .
4 a big boat
6 making people do hard work for low pay
7 a place where you buy things
8 opposite of 'off'
9 a place where ships unload their goods
13 the river in Liverpool
14 _____ birds
15 short for 'fabulous'
17 a glass container for fish and sea life
18 a performance by a pop group

Down

1 the time when you are a child
2 a bus with two floors
4 the horizon
5 Mars is a _____ .
10 a tourist trip by bus, car or boat
11 a house, office block, church, etc.
12 a boat that regularly carries people from one place to another
16 a musical group

* What is it in your language?
Find out!

What is being British?

When you walk along the streets of British cities you can see a multicultural* mix of people. At school your classmates are from different cultures and you learn to work together and make friends. So what does it mean to be a British teenager? And what do British teenagers think about Britain? Read about four teenagers' lives.

Saquib

My mum and dad came over from Pakistan when they were little. We have a newspaper shop in Birmingham. We live above the shop. At home we speak Punjabi, but we speak English as well. We're Muslims* but we aren't very strict*. We eat Pakistani food, but I also like burgers and chips. I love Britain and being British. It's a cool country. Asian culture is really cool now, too. I like watching Bollywood films with my friends – they have great music and dancing.

Danielle

My family is Afro-Caribbean. My grandparents came over from Barbados. Dad manages a computer store and Mum's a secretary. I like watching TV, going shopping and listening to music. We eat traditional* food and play Caribbean music, but I prefer hip-hop music to Bob Marley and reggae*! When I go out with my black friends we sometimes talk a special language; no one else can understand it! I went to Barbados once to see my relatives*. I feel Caribbean when I'm with my family, but I'm proud* to be black and British.

Sam

My parents are from Oxford and we still live here. My dad works at the BMW car factory and my mum works in a hospital. I love English food – like Sunday roast*. But my favourite food isn't really English; it's pizza, burgers and curry*! I like playing computer games and watching TV. I'm a Christian*, but we don't go to church very often. My favourite sport is football – I play with my friends. When there's a football match, I support* England of course!

Donald

My family is Chinese. They came over to London in the 1950s. Mum and Dad have a Chinese restaurant in Chinatown. Mum and Dad want me to become a doctor but I want to study photography! I speak a bit of Chinese with my parents. We eat Chinese food at home, but I like going out for a pizza with my friends. We are Christians and we celebrate Chinese New Year. I love being British. I get a bit annoyed* if someone calls me Chinese, because I'm not, I was born here.

Write the names of people who ...

1 speak another language at home.

....

2 like watching modern Indian films.

....

3 like being British.

....

4 eat food from their culture at home.

....

5 like eating pizzas, burgers or chips.

....

6 speak more than one language.

....

7 speak a special language with friends.

....

8 want to be a photographer.

....

9 play football.

....

10 practise* a religion.

....

Put these words with the correct ethnic group.

black   Chinatown   reggae
Chinese New Year   Pakistan   Sunday roast
Barbados   Bob Marley   Punjabi
Muslim   Bollywood

Asian	Chinese

Afro Caribbean	White

MY FACTFILE

What about your culture?
Complete the Factfile about you.

Name:

....

My family is from:

....

Dad's job: ....

Mum's job: ....

We live in:

....

Nationality:

....

Religion:

....

Language:

....

We eat:

....

I listen to:

....

My favourite sport:

....

My favourite food:

....

When there's a football match,

I support:

....

I'm proud to be:

....

* What is it in your language? Find out!

A multicultural mix

Britain is a multicultural mix. It has a total population* of around 60 million and 4 million are non-white. The ethnic communities* come from all over the world. Let's check your geography first!

Number the countries.

.... Europe

.... Australia

.... North America

.... Central America
and the Caribbean

.... South America

.... Asia

.... Africa

Large ethnic groups in the UK come from the following countries. Do you know what regions of the world they are in? Write a number from the map for each country.

Then use the bold letters to find another Asian country with a large ethnic group in the UK.

☐ Al**b**ania ☐ Som**a**lia ☐ I**n**dia ☐ U**g**anda ☐ Italy

☐ **J**amaica ☐ Polan**d** ☐ th**e** USA ☐ Paki**s**tan

☐ **C**hina ☐ T**r**inidad

B _ _ _ _ _ _ _ _ _

This pie chart tells you how many people come from the different ethnic groups.

How's your maths? Answer the questions.

1 Which group is biggest? ....

2 Which groups are smallest? ....

3 Which group is half a million? ....

4 Which group is just over half a million? ....

5 Which group is just under half a million? ....

Pie chart:
- Chinese 200,000
- black African 400,000
- black Caribbean 500,000
- Bangladeshi 200,000
- Pakistani 600,000
- Indian 900,000
- Other groups 900,000

Did you know?
Nearly 300 languages are spoken in London.

British (and American) teenagers have their own slang*.
Look at these new words and expressions. Many of them come from the hip-hop music scene.

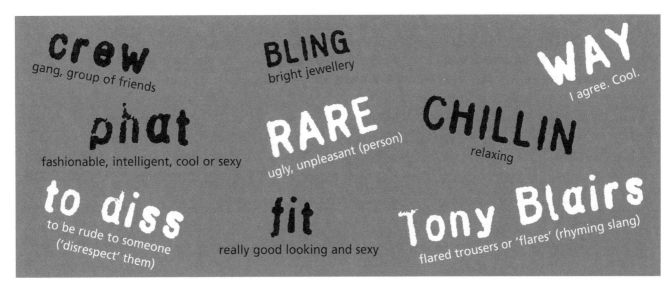

crew gang, group of friends

BLING bright jewellery

WAY I agree. Cool.

phat fashionable, intelligent, cool or sexy

RARE ugly, unpleasant (person)

CHILLIN relaxing

to diss to be rude to someone ('disrespect' them)

fit really good looking and sexy

Tony Blairs flared trousers or 'flares' (rhyming slang)

Complete what these teenagers are saying.

1. What are you doing?

I'm just .... with my ....

2. What do you think of my .... ?

They're really .... !

3. I love him. He's so ....

You're joking! I think he's ....

4. You listen to rubbish music.

Don't .... me!

* What is it in your language? Find out!

The Asian influence

In the last ten years young Asian actors, comedians* and musicians have transformed the British public's ideas about the Asian community*. People enjoy Asian films and music and watch Asian comedians on TV.

Asian films – Bollywood

Bollywood is a word made from Bombay and Hollywood. It refers* to modern Indian cinema. It is the most popular type of film on the planet and is very successful in the UK. Bollywood makes more films than Hollywood and sells more tickets too. The films are full of songs, Indian dance routines*, comedy and action. The actors and actresses wear beautiful costumes, and there is always a love story, but lovers rarely* even kiss! The stars in Bollywood films become very rich and famous.

Asian music – Bangra

Bangra was originally Indian folk music which celebrated the harvest season. It has a heavy drum beat and folk singing and gets people dancing. It is very popular now in the UK, not only with Asians but also with young people generally. Bangra is sung in Bollywood movies and it has influenced a whole generation of pop and dance musicians.

Asian comedy – *Goodness Gracious Me*

Young Asian comedians are now very popular in the UK. One comedy programme called *Goodness Gracious Me* is series of sketches* about the Indian community in the UK. The characters are very funny. There is an Indian mother who always says 'I can make it at home for nothing', and a Bollywood superstar, Mr Chunky La Funga, who always upsets* his girlfriends. The themes are universal and make everyone laugh.

Asian chat show – *The Kumars at No 42*

The Kumars are a very funny Asian family who have their own home TV studio at number 42. They have famous people as their guests, including Richard E Grant and Jerry Hall. The guest rings the doorbell and goes into the house to the studio. The son, Sanjeev, who believes he is very good-looking, hosts* the show. There is a granny, who asks very personal questions, a father who is only interested in money, and a mother who always offers food. The famous guests never know what question will come next! It is very popular, and it has won lots of awards.

Now decide if the sentences are true (T) or false (F).
 1 Bollywood makes more money than Hollywood. ....
 2 Bollywood actors become famous for their passionate* love scenes. ....
 3 Bangra is a kind of food eaten at harvest festivals. ....
 4 Bangra is only popular with Asians. ....
 5 *Goodness Gracious Me* is about all the ethnic* communities in the UK. ....
 6 Mr Chunky La Funga is an actor but he isn't successful with women. ....
 7 The Kumars at No 42 are a comic* Asian family with a TV studio. ....
 8 The Kumars invite famous people but they never go on the show. ....
 9 The granny in the Kumar family is only interested in money. ....
10 *The Kumars at No 42* is a very successful show. ....

Tell your partner what you think.
Would you like to ...
      see a Bollywood film?   Sure   Not sure
      listen to Bangra?   Sure   Not sure
      see Mr Chunky La Funga?   Sure   Not sure
      meet the Kumars?   Sure   Not sure

Asian words

Asian culture has influenced the English language for centuries.
Match the words with their definitions and then write the words above the pictures.

bungalow   a flat crunchy* bread
pyjamas   we burn these to make a nice smell
bindi   dark eye make-up
poppadom   jewellery we wear on our wrists
curry   a sweet-sour* jam
joss sticks   a beautiful dress that Asian women wear
chutney   a house with one floor
sari   a small spot Asian women wear on their forehead
bangle   a spicy dish we eat with rice
kohl   clothes we wear in bed

Which word do you think has been in English since the 16th century?
Clue – there are many restaurants that sell it in England. And it can be delivered to your house.

 * What is it in your language? Find out!

Football fun

Read the facts about football and write these headings in the correct places.

Pub football   English rules!   We are the champions!

Sex symbol   It's old!   It's popular!

1 ....

Richard II banned* the game in the 14th century because it was so dangerous. Football became* really popular in the 19th century.

4 ....

There are more than 50,000 football clubs in the UK. Over 240 million people in more than 200 countries play football just for fun! More people watch football matches in football stadiums* or on TV.

2 ....

English fans* remember when England were the champions in the World Cup at Wembley in 1966. In the 2004 World Cup, millions of English people put the St George's flag on their cars. But they didn't win!

5 ....

A new British tradition is watching important matches at the pub on big screens.

3 ....

George Best was the world's first football sex symbol* in the 1960s! David Beckham, an English player, is a fashion icon* all over the world.

6 ....

Although it's an international game, England made the rules. That's why football pitches all over the world are measured in yards and not metres.

Play the game and find the name of an English football player. Circle the coordinates* next to the correct ending of each sentence and find the letters on the football pitch.

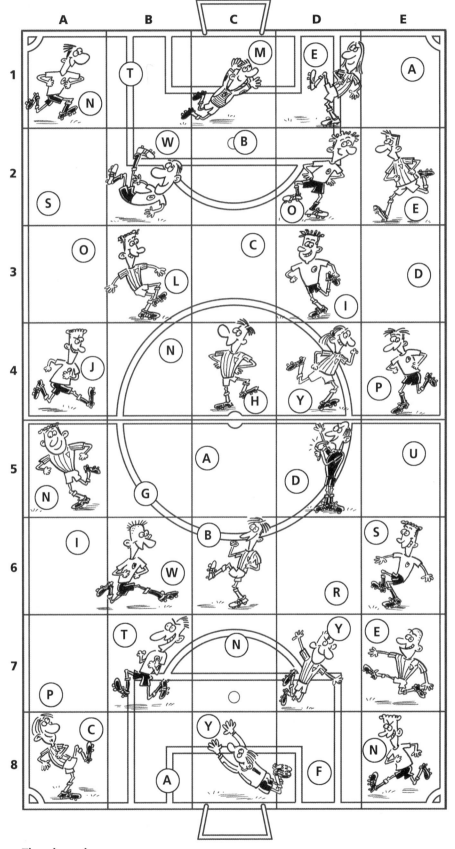

1 The score is …
the points per team. **2B**
the number of players. **1E**

2 The goalkeeper …
is the manager. **1A**
stops goals*. **1E**

3 A pitch is …
the playing field. **4D**
the first kick of the ball. **5A**

4 A team has …
eleven players. **5A**
twenty-two players. **2C**

5 The kick off is …
the first kick of the match. **7E**
the last kick of the match. **3C**

6 The referee …
takes the tickets. **4A**
controls* the game. **6D**

7 Training means …
exercise and practice. **2D**
travelling to the match. **6B**

8 Half time is …
the score after 45 minutes. **8A**
a break* after 45 minutes
of play. **3A**

9 Fans are …
air-conditioning*. **6B**
the followers* of a team. **1A**

10 To chant means …
to sing a special football song. **2E**
to lose a match. **6D**

11 The coach …
pays all the players. **8B**
trains the players. **8C**

The player is …
1__ 2__ 3__ 4__ 5__ 6__ 7__ 8__ 9__ 10__ 11__ ,
the youngest footballer to score for England.
Who are your favourite football teams and players?

* **What is it in your language?**
Find out!

Crazy about cricket

Read the interview and match the questions and answers. Then complete the sentence at the bottom of the page with the letters at the end of each answer.

Did you know?
- Top cricketers are very famous in the UK.
- Professional cricketers earn a lot of money.
- The cricket ball goes very fast and it's very hard too!

Meet Tim McDowell, a young cricket professional*.

1 What's so exciting about cricket?

2 Isn't cricket just for the English?

3 When did it start?

4 So is cricket really old-fashioned?

5 Do you have to be fit?

6 Is cricket easy to understand?

7 Has it got a lot of strange words and expressions?

8 What's your advice* for young cricket players?

a It started in 1300 – so that's a long time ago! **E**

b No, it isn't. It's got a traditional* image, but it's changing all the time. These days, players often wear coloured clothes and the fans* are really noisy! I think it's becoming more like American baseball. **A**

c No way! Cricket is played all over the world from the West Indies to Australia, and from India to Italy. It's an international sport. **H**

d Well, the rules are a bit complicated*, but it isn't that difficult. **H**

e Yes, it has – things like a 'duck', a 'maiden over', a 'wicket' and a 'yorker'. I won't try to explain them. **E**

f You have to be very fit to be a modern professional player. We train as hard as athletes*. **S**

g It's exciting because games can change very quickly. One moment you think you're winning, and the next moment you're losing! It's an amazing sport. **T**

h Go out and play and have a great time! **S**

England and Australia are great cricket rivals*. Every two years they try to win 1__ 2__ 3__ 4__ 5__ 6__ 7__ 8__ .

A simple guide to cricket!

- There are two teams of eleven players. One team bats and the other bowls (or throws) and fields*.
- The batting side has two players on the pitch, the fielding side has eleven players.
- The team with the ball bowls the ball. The player who bowls is called a 'bowler'.

- The team with the bat hits the ball. The player is called a 'batsman'.
- The batting team tries to score 'runs' or points.
- The fielders (the other players in the bowling side) try to get the batsmen out by hitting the wicket (three sticks in the ground) or catching the ball.
- The team with the most points wins.

Label the picture with these words. | fielder   wicket   batsman   cricket ball   bowler   cricket pitch   cricket bat

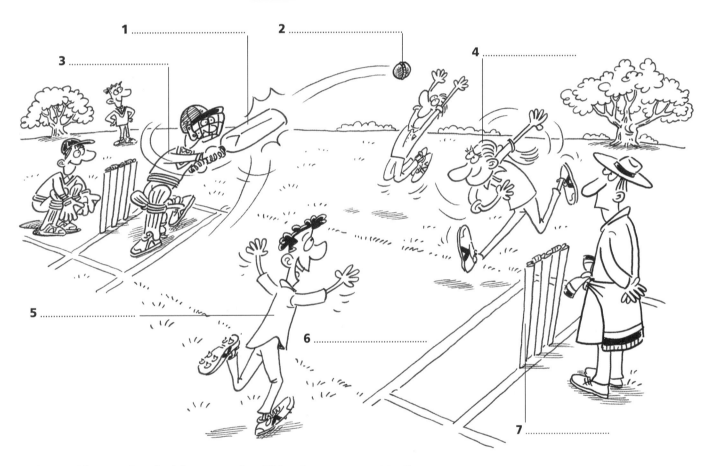

1 ....

2 ....

3 ....

4 ....

5 ....

6 ....

7 ....

These cricketers played cricket yesterday. Write the names next to the scores.

Bob didn't get as many runs as Julia.
Ray got more runs than Bob and Julia.
Agnes got fewer runs than Ray and Paul.
Julia got more runs than one player.
Paul got more runs than Agnes.
Ray got more runs than three other players.

.... 100

.... 90

.... 70

.... 40

.... 20

* What is it in your language? Find out!

Rugby mania

Rugby facts

- **Confusing** There are two different kinds of rugby – Rugby Union and Rugby League.
- **International** Top Rugby Union countries are Australia, England, France, Italy, New Zealand, South Africa, Scotland, Ireland and Wales.
- **Strange shape** The shape of a rugby ball makes it easy to carry.
- **National heroes** Nowadays rugby players are extremely famous. Crowds of young people greet the players at airports. Jonny Wilkinson is a sex symbol.
- **A rugby scrum** Rugby is a very physical* game. When you see the players all together with their heads down, it's called a scrum.
- **Two halves** The game is played in two 40 minute halves with a 10-minute break at half time.
- **Men and women** It's a game played by women, too. There are a lot of women's rugby teams at universities.

Did you know?

This famous chant started at rugby matches. Can you chant it?

Oggy, oggy, oggy!
Oi, oi, oi!
Oggy, oggy, oggy!
Oi, oi, oi!

Put the sentences in order and write the letters at the end of the sentences to answer the question below.

How many rugby players are there in a team?
1__ 2__ 3__ 4__ 5__ 6__ 7__

A Very Short History of Rugby

- ◯ In 1871 the Rugby Football Union created the rules for the new game. **T**
- ◯ The teachers thought that William's idea was an improvement* to the game. **F**
- ◯ Rugby Union waited another hundred years to become professional! **N**
- ◯ The game of rugby started by accident* at Rugby school in 1823. **F**
- ◯ During a game of football at Rugby School, a 16-year-old called William Webb Ellis picked up the ball and started running with it. **I**
- ◯ In the same year as that first international match, Rugby League became a professional game. **E**
- ◯ In 1895, Scotland and England played the first international Rugby League match – Scotland won. **E**

Read about Jonny Wilkinson.

Name: Jonny Wilkinson
Born: 25 May, 1979, England
Height: 1.78 metres
Weight: 85 kilograms
Hobbies: cinema, good food, tennis, football
Pre-match ritual*: always wears the same T-shirt under his England shirt
2003: received an MBE[1] in the New Year's honour lists[2]
2004: received an OBE[1]

Rugby is a tough physical game, and players need to have the right equipment*.
Look at the picture and match the descriptions with the kit and equipment.

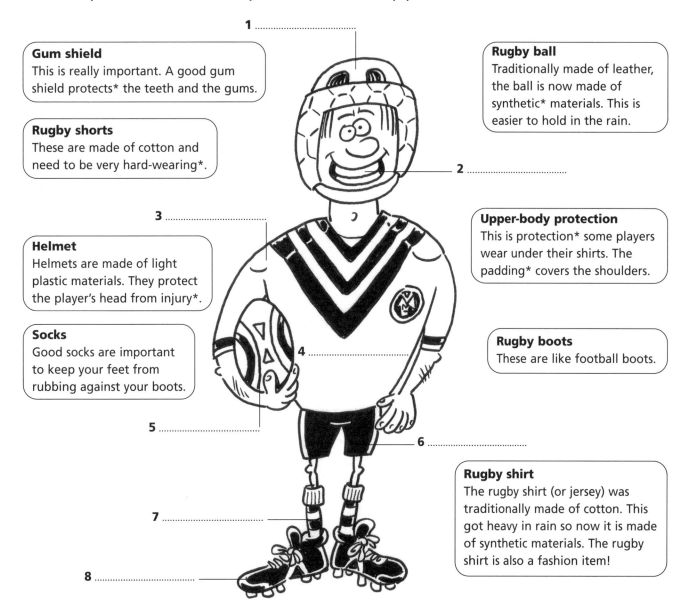

Gum shield
This is really important. A good gum shield protects* the teeth and the gums.

Rugby shorts
These are made of cotton and need to be very hard-wearing*.

Helmet
Helmets are made of light plastic materials. They protect the player's head from injury*.

Socks
Good socks are important to keep your feet from rubbing against your boots.

Rugby ball
Traditionally made of leather, the ball is now made of synthetic* materials. This is easier to hold in the rain.

Upper-body protection
This is protection* some players wear under their shirts. The padding* covers the shoulders.

Rugby boots
These are like football boots.

Rugby shirt
The rugby shirt (or jersey) was traditionally made of cotton. This got heavy in rain so now it is made of synthetic materials. The rugby shirt is also a fashion item!

Think of a sport you play. Write a description of the kit and equipment.

Divide the class into two teams. One student is the quiz master and asks these questions. Score two points per correct answer.

Class rugby match

1 What was the name of the boy who started rugby?
2 How old was he?
3 What are the two types of rugby played today?
4 How many rugby players are there in a team?
5 Why isn't a rugby ball round?
6 When all the players are together with their heads down, what is it called?
7 Name four top rugby countries.
8 How long is a rugby game?
9 Chant the rugby chant.
10 What was a rugby ball originally made of?
11 What year was Jonny Wilkinson born in?
12 What does he do to have good luck?

Glossary: [1]An MBE (Member of the Order of the British Empire), and [2]OBE (Officer of the Order of the British Empire) are [3]New year's Honours titles given by the Queen on New Year's Day.

* What is it in your language? Find out!

Why not watch a rugby match? You might enjoy it!

The 1950s and 1960s

At the start of the 1950s, most people didn't have TVs, teenage clothes were boring and music was old-fashioned. But things changed quickly! By the 1960s London was the style and music capital of the world. What do you know about the 1950s and 1960s? Try this quiz!

1 Which person wasn't in The Beatles?
a) John Lennon **b)** Keith Richards **c)** Ringo Starr

2 Which word was new in the 1950s?
a) teenager **b)** boyfriend **c)** cool

3 What was a new way to listen to music in the 1960s?
a) cassette player **b)** Walkman **c)** record player

4 Where was the trendy* place to meet friends the 1950s?
a) the coffee bar **b)** the shopping centre **c)** the disco

5 Which British band had hits in the 1960s?
a) Dire Straits **b)** The Rolling Stones **c)** Iron Maiden

6 Which 1960s British band came from London?
a) The Where **b)** The What **c)** The Who

7 What was a new women's fashion item* in the 1960s?
a) the mini skirt **b)** the bikini **c)** jeans

8 What new fashion item did the film stars Marlon Brando and James Dean wear in the 1950s?
a) the sweatshirt **b)** the T-shirt **c)** the sweater

8-10 points: You are a pop & fashion expert*!
4-7 points: You know a lot about the past!
0-3 points: You live in the present!

SCORE
One point for a correct answer:
1 b **2** a **3** a **4** a **5** b **6** c **7** a **8** b

Music

The Rolling Stones and The Beatles were the top two British bands of the 1960s.
Read about the bands. Which band is which? Write the band names in the correct places.

The Rolling Stones

The Beatles

.... changed pop music
forever! During the 1960s the 'Fab Four' had 21 Top Ten
singles* in the UK. Thousands of teenage girls went to
their concerts. In 1965, they had five singles in the
American charts* … at number five, four, three, two
and one! John Lennon and Paul McCartney wrote nearly
all their songs, including *Yesterday* and *Help!*

Teenagers' parents didn't like ....
This band was shocking*. Their concerts were very
exciting. Mick Jagger and Keith Richards wrote a lot of
their famous songs, such as *Satisfaction*. They are still
making music today!

Style

Match the pictures with the descriptions. Then label the pictures.

leather jacket skirt suit jeans
sandals trousers motorbike
jewellery scooter tie jacket

*What is it in your language?
Find out!

1950s Teddy Boys … ....
wore tight* trousers, narrow* ties
and long jackets.

1960s Mods … ....
had short hair, wore suits, and
rode scooters.

1960s Rockers … ....
wore leather jackets and jeans and
rode motorbikes.

1960s Hippies … ....
had long hair, wore flared* jeans or
long skirts, lots of ethnic* jewellery
and sandals*.

The 1970s and 1980s

There were huge changes in fashion and music in the 1970s and 1980s. Teenagers spent a lot of money on new fashions. They bought the latest music and followed the charts* every week. In the 1980s, CDs and videos changed the way people listened to music. The most popular music of the 1970s was disco and soul* from the USA, while from the UK came glam and punk.

Read about glam and punk and decide where these sentences go.

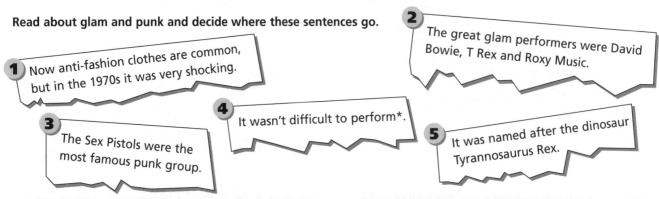

1 Now anti-fashion clothes are common, but in the 1970s it was very shocking.

2 The great glam performers were David Bowie, T Rex and Roxy Music.

3 The Sex Pistols were the most famous punk group.

4 It wasn't difficult to perform*.

5 It was named after the dinosaur Tyrannosaurus Rex.

Glam rock

Glam was short for glamorous. [ ] They wore make-up, jewellery, platform* boots and colourful clothes. David Bowie's greatest glam album* was *The Rise and Fall of Ziggy Stardust and the Spiders from Mars* (and it was one of the longest titles ever!). T Rex was a glam rock band. [ ] Their lead singer was Marc Bolan. He wrote strange rock songs. He died in a car crash. The lead singer of Roxy Music was Bryan Ferry.

There are two different *God save the Queen*s! One is the British national anthem*, the other is the Sex Pistols' song. The song came out in 1977. The BBC refused* to play it, many shops refused to sell it – but it still went to number 2 in the British charts!

Punk

Punk songs were fast, aggressive* … and short! [ ] Their lead singer was Johnny Rotten – but their guitarist Sid Vicious became the great symbol* of punk. Other big bands were The Clash and The Stranglers. They wore anti-fashion clothes: work boots, black leather, torn* clothes with safety pins*, chains and badges. [ ] Punks wore makeup and had colourful Mohican haircuts or shaved* heads. The great punk dance was Pogo dancing. [ ] You simply jumped up and down!

Which do you prefer punk or glam?
Are there any glam or punk bands today?
Do you like them?
Do you wear any clothes today that are like these clothes?

Unscramble these words from the article and match them to the pictures.
Then write G (Glam) or P (Punk) or GP (Glam and Punk) for each item.

a ○

1 c i h a o n m c a u t h i r

2 f o m t l a r p s o b o t

3 t n o r c o l t s e h

4 k r o w t o b s o

b ○

5 e f s t a y n i p

6 i a e g r r n

c ○

7 p e a k u m –

8 i h a c n   d ○

e ○   f ○

9 g e b d a

g ○   h ○   i ○

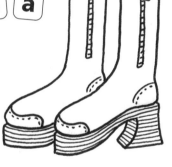

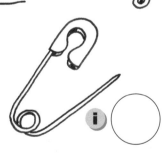

Did you know?

'Vicious' means aggressive and 'rotten' means bad or horrible (for example, fresh food goes rotten). Sid Vicious changed his name from John Simon Richie and Johnny Rotten changed his name from John Lydon. Why do you think they chose these new names? Do you know any other pop stars or actors who changed their names?

What were their real names?

1 Elton John   a David Jones
2 David Bowie   b Georgios Kyriacos
3 Boy George   c Reginald Dwight
4 George Michael   d George O'Dowd

Which one totally changed his name?

Answers: 1 c 2 a 3 d 4 b

* What is it in your language? Find out!

The 1990s to today

Lots of new bands appeared* in the 1990s and Hip-hop or Rap came over from the United States. Read about this decade and complete the sentences on the right.

Westlife

Boy bands

Boybands like Westlife, East 17 and Boyzone were huge in the 1990s. They were good-looking, wore nice clothes and sang nice songs. Kids, teenagers and their parents liked them. Music managers created them and wrote their songs. The most successful band was Take That. After the band split up*, Robbie Williams became an international star.

Girl power

Music managers created girl bands too. The biggest girl band was The Spice Girls. A music manager chose five young women and gave them new songs and nicknames* – Ginger, Posh, Scary, Sporty and Baby. Each girl had her own style and everyone had their favourite. Their message was 'girl power' – girls can do what they want. Their first single, *Wannabee*, went straight to number 1 in the UK charts and was a hit in 21 other countries.

Britpop

Oasis and Blur were the two biggest new British bands in the 1990s. They wrote their own songs. They became rivals* like The Beatles and The Rolling Stones in the 1960s. But don't forget Radiohead, Travis and Coldplay. These were the next generation of top British bands!

Hip-hop and garage

Hip-hop or Rap started in the mid 1970s in the USA. Rap included street poetry and disco. Hip-hop influenced British pop culture in the 1990s and there were many hip-hop groups in London. Ms Dynamite is the most famous hip-hop artist to come from the UK. Garage music also became big in the 1990s with its strong bass beat*.

Pop idol

In 2001 there was a new kind of TV programme called *Pop Idol*. The public loved this competition for hopeful* teenage singers and enjoyed listening to the judges' comments. More than 13 million people watched the final of the first series and there were 8.7 million phone votes. The winners became famous overnight*. The winner in 2002 was Will Young.

Complete the sentences. Use the passive form of these verbs.

watch write choose influence
like compare create

1 Boybands .... by both parents and their kids.

2 Boy and girl bands .... by music managers.

3 Five young women .... to be in The Spice Girls.

4 Oasis and Blur songs .... by the group members.

5 Oasis and Blur .... to The Beatles and The Rolling Stones.

6 In the 1990s, British pop culture .... by hip-hop.

7 The final of the first Pop Idol series .... by 13 million people.

Do you like boy and girl bands? Posh is still on the front pages of newspapers and magazines worldwide. Why? What's her new name?
Do you like hip-hop or garage? Would you like to enter a competition like Pop Idol?

Who are the new tribes*? What do they wear? What do they listen to? Some recent surveys found these tribes in Britain, but watch out! Things change VERY quickly!

Can you match the tribes to the pictures and fill in the form below?

Goths ....
The Goth colour is black. Everything is black! Their hair, their clothes, their fingernails*. They even wear black lipstick! But their faces are often covered in white make-up. They wear long black coats. They like Marilyn Manson, but The Cure are the best band ever!

Nu-Metallers ....
They listen to bands like Limp Bizkit and Blink 182. They like hip-hop, and they like it loud! They wear T-shirts of their favourite bands. And they often have lots of piercings* in their ears, lips and eyebrows.

Grungers ....
Along with the Goths, they are the oldest of the tribes. They love Nirvana, of course – Kurt Cobain is the king! They don't wear expensive clothes. They like trainers, jeans with holes in them, old T-shirts, hooded sweatshirts ('hoodies') and blond dreadlocks*.

Gangstas ....
They love rap and hip-hop. Their favourite stars are Eminem and Destiny's Child. They wear designer sportswear and lots of jewellery ('bling'). They've got a lot of 'attitude'*.

Pop Princesses ....
Pink, pink, pink! It's the best colour of their clothes, shoes, mobile phones ... everything! And they like lots of silver jewellery. They watch the Pop Idol TV series and they love Will Young and Gareth Gates. Their queen of pop is Britney Spears!

	Goths	Nu-Metallers	Grungers	Gangstas	Pop Princesses
colour					
clothes					
body decoration, hairstyles, jewellery					
favourite bands, singers					

* What is it in your language? Find out!

The seaside

British people love going to the seaside. There is so much to see and do even if the weather isn't great. Let's find out more about the seaside. Look at the clues and label the picture.

1 A **jellyfish** is a sea animal. It can be dangerous.

2 You wear **flippers** on your feet. They help you swim faster.

3 You catch fish with a **fishing net**.

4 You use a **surf board** to surf.

5 A **starfish** is a sea animal. It looks like a star.

6 You use a **beach towel** after you swim to dry yourself.

7 **Shells** are beautiful objects and the homes of shellfish.

8 A **crab** is a sea animal with 8 legs and two big arms. You can eat it.

9 You wear a **mask** on your face.

10 **Pebbles** are small round stones you find on the beach.

11 **Mussels** are small black shellfish. You can eat them.

12 You sit on a **deck chair** on the beach.

13 You put a **snorkel** in your mouth so you can breathe under water.

14 **Seaweed** is a sea plant – it grows in the sea.

15 You wear a **wetsuit** to keep you warm in the sea.

Read the article and write the missing words.
swimming beach student boring surfer clean Cornwall trouble games

Beach life!

This week, we're talking to Steve Anderson, a life guard at Perranporth, Cornwall.

You've got a great job, Steve!
Yeah, it's fun. I meet lots of people. And I'm outside*
all the time – so when it's a nice day, it's brilliant*.
But it isn't like *Baywatch*. We're in
a) .... , not California!

What do you like about the job?
I meet lots of girls. I like that. And I really like talking
to the surfers. I'm a **b)** ...., too, and
I love hearing their stories.

Are there any bad things?
Oh sure! It can be a bit **c)** ....
And people do some silly things. Sometimes they
swim too far from the beach and they get into
d) .... I have to swim out to help
them. Sometimes they float* a long way from the
beach on air beds. I use jet skis to get to them
quickly. And people drop rubbish on the **e)**
.... I tell them to pick it up.
It's important to keep the beach **f)** ....

Do the British love seaside holidays?
Oh yeah! They come down in the morning and they
stay all day! They bring picnics, books, newspapers,
g) .... and beach umbrellas. They
bring jumpers and jackets, too. It can get cold on
the beach in an English summer!

**What was your most frightening* moment
this year?**
Well, I saw a shark about a month ago.
It was very close!

And the most exciting?
h) .... with dolphins! They were
really beautiful.

What do you do in the winter?
Actually, I'm a **i)** .... I'm studying
science at university. This is just a summer job.

Where are you studying?
At Sussex University in Brighton. I'm near the sea
all year, so that's great!

**Read the article again and put the
pictures in order.**

* What is it in your language?
Find out!

On the river

The British love playing around in boats. And if they aren't very near the sea – well, there's always the river!

Can you name these boats? (yacht   ferry   rowing boat   canoe   barge   power boat   dinghy)

1 ....

2 ....

3 ....

4 ....

5 ....

6 ....

7 ....

Read about the races and match the photos with the descriptions.

RACING ON THE RIVER

a

b

c

1 Oxford Cambridge Boat Race, River Thames, March

This world-famous race in London is between England's two oldest universities. Rowing teams from each university race against each other. Millions of people watch it.

2 Henley Royal Regatta, River Thames, June

This is the oldest river regatta in the world and started in 1839. It lasts for five days. The races are a mile long and go against the flow* of the river! There are 100 races. Some people still wear traditional* 19th century clothes.

3 Great River Race, River Thames, September

There are lots of strange boats in the most spectacular* race on the Thames. They include Chinese dragon boats, Hawaiian war* canoes and Viking longboats!

Write the names of the races.

1 It's between two universities: ....

2 There are boats from all over the world: ....

3 It's a very old race: ....

Did you know?

'Regatta' is an Italian word.
It means a Venetian gondola race

It's always nice to live near the water. We talked to teenagers who live by rivers.
What do they like about it?

Oxford

I live in the university city, Oxford. We have an unusual home – it's a houseboat on a canal* in the city centre. You have to look hard to find us! We have an address like other people and a letter box. I live with my mum, dad and brother. It isn't very big, but it's got everything. There's a living room, a kitchen and bathroom. I've got a very small bedroom. I love it. I can feed the ducks from my window.
Kim

Stratford upon Avon

I live in Stratford-upon-Avon – the birthplace* of William Shakespeare. As the name tells you, it is on the River Avon. I live in a big house, with my mum, dad and sister. Our garden is by the river and we have a little boat. I learnt to row* when I was small and I still love rowing. We also go running along the river. It's fun. We get up early on Saturday morning – that's hard in the winter – but we see animals and birds, and the seasons changing – it's lovely.
Serena

Glasgow

I live in Glasgow in Scotland, on the River Clyde. My mum, my brother and our dog live in a modern flat with a balcony*. I go canoeing once a week with the canoeing club. We usually go on the Forth and Clyde canal in the city centre. The Clyde is quite dangerous because it's near the sea so the water sometimes flows* quite fast. At the weekend we walk the dog along the Clyde – it's like being in the country.
Robert

Liverpool

I live in a small house with my mum, dad and two sisters in Liverpool on the River Mersey. My favourite free-time activity is fishing. I often go out all day with my friends to the river bank*. We don't catch many fish! When friends visit we go on the Mersey ferry. You can see the city from the river. In summer there's a river festival with music, street shows, and water sports – windsurfing, jet skiing, sailing and canoeing.
Gavin

Now decide if these sentences are true (T) or false (F).

1 Kim travels from town to town in a boat. ....
2 Robert has got a dog. ....
3 Gavin takes the ferry to school every day. ....
4 Serena often goes running. ....
5 Oxford is on the River Mersey. ....
6 The River Clyde is in England. ....
7 Liverpool has a river festival. ....
8 Shakespeare came from Stratford-upon-Avon. ....

Which place would you like to visit? Why?
Is there a river near your home?
Do you do any activities near or on the river?

* What is it in your language? Find out!

The seaside resort

Do you think it's cold and rainy in the summer in Britain and that British people don't swim in the sea? Well, you're wrong! Britain is an island and it's got a lot of coastline* with beautiful beaches and seaside resorts. And the weather isn't that bad, you know!

Read about the resorts and write their names under the pictures.

1

....

- a pier
- luxury hotels
- gardens
- language schools

2

....

- a pier
- decorative lights
- a famous tower
- a theme park

3

....

- beautiful coastline
- water sports
- lots of surfing
- nightclubs

Illuminating* Blackpool

This traditional resort is in the North of England, and it is still very popular today. It's got a pier, the famous Blackpool tower, and wide sandy beaches with lots of fun things to do. In the autumn don't miss the illuminations – amazing, decorative* street lights. These can even be seen from space! Blackpool Pleasure Beach is a massive* theme park on the beach with brilliant rides. And the good news is that it's free to get in. You only have to pay for the rides!

Study English in Bournemouth

This is a resort in the South of England. Bournemouth has a good climate* with lots of sunshine and lovely sandy beaches. There is a pier, beautiful gardens, and lots of accommodation*, including luxury hotels. Although it is considered a place where old people go to retire*, it's also a place for the young. Bournemouth is the top European destination* for students studying English outside London. There are lots of language schools to choose from. So what are you waiting for?

Surf capital – Newquay

Cornwall is a top holiday destination because it has lots of sunshine, fantastic beaches and beautiful scenery*. It also has big waves from the Atlantic. Newquay is the most popular resort in Cornwall and it is the UK surf capital. Beginners can take surfing lessons, while surfing fans* can watch the world surfing championships. If you want a break from your surfboard*, why not try water skiing, windsurfing, or parascending*? And in the evening you can hang out in the town's trendy bars and nightclubs.

**Imagine you are in one of the seaside towns.
Write a postcard home.**

Complete these holiday confessions with the following words.

sea   girlfriend   holiday   parascending   cloudy   camping   tent
tough   fell   sailing   Spain   good   trouble   seals

My worst holiday ever!

Last year, I went on a **1** .... holiday in South Wales. It was August,

but in Britain that doesn't guarantee **2** .... weather. The first day

was cold and **3** .... but dry, and we put up the **4** ....

After that, it rained every day. In fact, it rained every day for two weeks!

We did a few nice things like watching **5** .... and going on a

boat. But I argued a lot with my sister, and I got into **6** ....

with my parents. So what are we doing this year? We're going to

sunny **7** .... !

Andy

My best holiday ever!

This summer, I went on an adventure **8** .... in Scotland.

It was amazing. I stayed in a big country house by the **9** ....

I learnt to surf, but I **10** .... in the sea a lot! I went scuba diving.

I went **11** .... on the sea – and there was a storm!

I went mountain biking (that was **12** ....). I learnt archery,

just like Robin Hood! And I went **13** .... It was the most

exciting thing I have ever done. And there was one other good thing.

I met my **14** .... , Alicia, there!

Tom

Whose holiday? Write A for Andy or T for Tom on the holiday photos.

What's your ideal holiday? What activities would you do?

* What is it in your language? Find out!

What's on this week?

**Want to go out this week? There's so much to do if you know where to go.
Read the guide and answer the questions.**

Oxygen
Your local multiplex cinema

Up to 9 different films showing at any one time
Big comfortable seats
15 metre screens
Digital sound system
Under 14s only £5.00

Concept Dance club
Tuesday: Under 18s night
Thursday: Weekly student event
Friday: Garage and house music
Saturday: Chart* and dance anthems*

Zodiac
The venue* for live music.
Different acts every week.
Dancing on Wednesday and
Thursday nights!
Hip-hop, Garage, Bangra, R & B

Nice ice
- The coolest place to have fun
- Olympic-sized ice rink*
- Family time 10.00 am to
  1.00 pm weekends
- DJ classics* Thursday

The Riverside Leisure Centre
13-screen cinema
4 restaurants
2 bars

Pizza City

• Enjoy our hospitality*
• 25 different sorts of pizza
• Special price before 7.00 pm
• Modern décor* with a fun atmosphere*

THE RED LION
A traditional pub with good beers,
relaxing* atmosphere,
good food and live Irish music.
Pub quiz every Tuesday.*

HOLLYWOOD ARENA
26-lane bowling alley* Bar and food area
Excellent fun for all!

Where can you ...

1 see live bands? ....
2 watch films? ....
3 play a game? ....
4 eat something? ....
   ....
5 pay less if it's early? ....

6 choose from a variety* of places to eat?
   ....
7 go ice-skating? ....
8 dance ....
9 go dancing if you are under 18? ....

Where can you go out in your town?

What's showing at Oxygen this week? Write the type of film under the posters.

| detective | horror | romantic | action | cartoon | historical | comedy | musical | science fiction |

....

....

....

....

....

....

....

....

....

Can you put this dialogue in order?

( ) No, I'm afraid not. The doors open in ten minutes.

( ) OK. That's £10, please.

( ) Here you are.

( ) We're both thirteen.

( ) Thanks. Can we go in yet?

( ) Yes, of course. How old are you?

( ) Can I have two tickets for the film on Screen 5, please?

( ) Thanks. Here are your tickets.

Practise the dialogue with a partner.

* What is it in your language? Find out!

Places to go

These teenagers have reviewed places they visited. One problem – their scores have got lost.
What do you think their scores were? Colour in the number of stars.

★ terrible   ★★ not great   ★★★ OK   ★★★★ cool   ★★★★★ perfect

Oasis Water Fun Park

Last weekend we came here for the afternoon. The Acquaslide was brilliant. I went down it about ten times! It's really fast and you make a huge splash* as you hit the water. I liked the pool, too – and the wave machine was fantastic. Afterwards we went for a burger and I ate an enormous ice-cream! It was a good day out.

☆☆☆☆☆

Ryedale Folk Museum

Ryedale is an open air museum with lots of old houses and shops showing what English village life was like in the past. There was an 1800s cottage with ladies in traditional* clothes cooking bread over the fire. We went inside a cute gypsy caravan*, too! I learnt how to make a rug* and took it home with me. I had a great day but I wouldn't go again – there was no café and the shop wasn't great.

☆☆☆☆☆

Vote* for your favourite attractions!

Paintballing

I went paintballing with a group of my friends. It's the latest outdoor* game – you go out into the woods with a 'gun' that shoots paint balls. You chase each other and try to hit each other. If someone hits you with a paintball you get splashed with paint and lose a point. We got covered* in mud (and paint) but it was really exciting. You have to wear protective* clothes and a mask* because it hurts a bit when the paintball hits you. We were really tired at the end of the day.

☆☆☆☆☆

Paultons Park

We went to Paultons for the day. We went on some good rides. I liked the Wave Runner best. We sat in boats on fast-flowing* water and got really wet. On the Astroglide we sat on trays* and raced down the slides. That was great, too! My younger sister and her friend went on the Pirate boat and visited Dinosaur World. Mum made me go with them. I felt so stupid, especially* in the Flying Frog! It was a good day, but there wasn't really enough for people my age and the rides weren't scary enough.

☆☆☆☆☆

Look at the pictures and complete the crossword.
Find the name of another place to go? ....

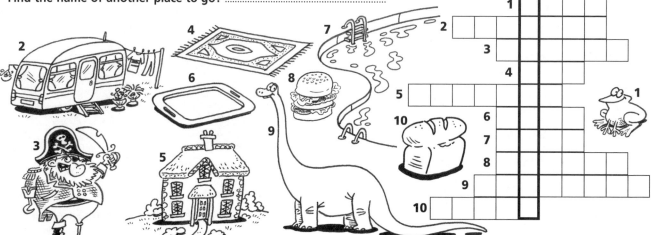

The pub

Think of Britain and you think of pubs! Pubs have always been the centre of social life and the place to go at lunchtime and in the evening. Although traditionally* they were for adults, nowadays they are often for families as well. And you can eat food or just have a drink.

Pub history

The Romans brought taverns* to England. These had memorable* names.
In the Middle Ages many people couldn't read, so the signs had pictures on them, too.
A pub was originally* called a public house. It was (and still is) a house with a licence* to sell alcohol*.
In the 17th century King James of Scotland ordered that a red lion should be put on every public house.

Match the beginnings and endings of the sentences to find out the facts.

Pub facts

1 Darts, billiards and dominoes	have live music.
2 'Pub grub' is	stand up and sing a song in an Irish pub.
3 A 'Gastro pub'	a slang term for pub food.
4 Going for a pub lunch	large-screen TVs and show big football matches.
5 Only people over 18	is a trendy pub serving high-quality* food.
6 You can find	can buy alcohol in a pub.
7 Pubs often	are traditional pub games.
8 Customers often	is a very popular* British activity.
9 Pubs often have	but you can't buy a drink there.
10 At 14 you can enter a pub	Irish pubs all over the world.

These pub names are the most common in the UK. Match them to the pub signs.

The Crown   The Royal Oak   The Swan   The Bell
The Ship   The Star   The White Horse   The Red Lion

1 ....

2 ....

3 ....

4 ....

5 ....

6 ....

7 ....

8 ....

* What is it in your language? Find out!

Meeting up

**What's the most popular free-time activity for British teenagers?
It's hanging out! And where do they do that? Read on and find out.**

**Tick the places where you think British
teenagers hang out.**

- ❑ the youth club
- ❑ school
- ❑ home
- ❑ the shopping centre
- ❑ the library
- ❑ the cinema
- ❑ the swimming pool
- ❑ the museum
- ❑ the park
- ❑ a fast food restaurant

Write the names of the places.

1 ....

There's a good skateboard park
and I'm a keen skateboarder.
We hang out and chat. We even
have a favourite bench*! We play
cricket in the summer and football
in the winter.
Mohammed, Bradford

2 ....

We often go on Saturday and
there's lots to do. We go shopping,
have a coffee, or just sit around
and chat.
Ella, Southampton

3 ....

We meet two evenings a week.
We just sit round and chat in the
lounge, watch sport on the TV or
play games – we've got two pool
tables and a table tennis table.
We're building an Internet
room at the moment.
Lewis, Dublin

4 ....

We go two evenings a week –
it's good fun. We've got a season
ticket. After swimming we hang
out in the café.
Olivia, Cardiff

5 ....

It's cheap and we can hang out
together. I love hamburgers, but
sometimes I have a salad to please
my mum!
Liam, Oxford

6 ....

We often go once or twice a month I go to the
multiplex with my friends and it's
my favourite place. We see all the
latest films. We always buy a big
box of popcorn. I love it!
Aaron, Canterbury

7 ....

We listen to music, read
magazines and talk about clothes
and make- up. Sometimes we
have a sleepover*. We watch
DVDs in my room and my
friends stay the night.
Jade, Manchester

Find the words and expressions in the report.

1 You buy this so you can do an activity as often as you

like. s............................... t...............................

2 You sit on this in a park or garden. b...............................

3 A kind of food made of corn. p...............................

4 A summer sport c...............................

5 A party when friends stay the night. s...............................

6 You can choose from lots of different films here.

m...............................

7 You go to this place to use your skateboard.

s............................... p...............................

8 This game is similar* to snooker. p...............................

Do you like doing any of these things ?

British teenagers often say that there isn't enough for them to do in their area.
Under-18s can't buy drinks in a pub, so they don't hang out there. So what do teenagers want?

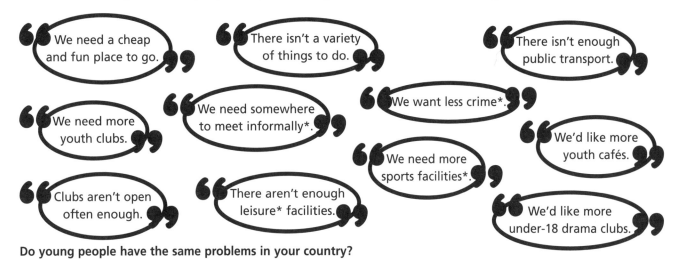

"We need a cheap and fun place to go."

"There isn't a variety of things to do."

"There isn't enough public transport."

"We need more youth clubs."

"We need somewhere to meet informally*."

"We want less crime*."

"We'd like more youth cafés."

"Clubs aren't open often enough."

"There aren't enough leisure* facilities."

"We need more sports facilities*."

"We'd like more under-18 drama clubs."

Do young people have the same problems in your country?

You are on a committee to create a youth club. You can only afford* six of the things below.
Work in groups and decide what you are going to buy and where you will put the new things.

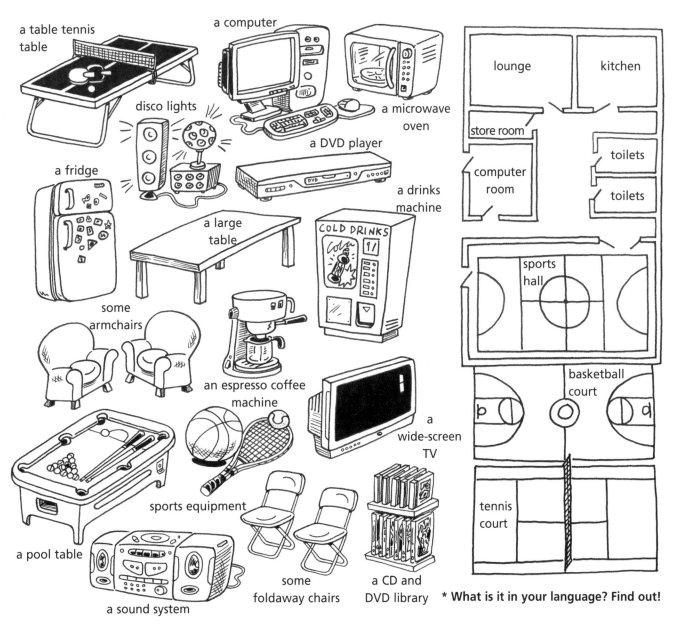

a table tennis table

a computer

a microwave oven

disco lights

a DVD player

a fridge

a drinks machine

a large table

some armchairs

an espresso coffee machine

a wide-screen TV

a pool table

sports equipment

some foldaway chairs

a CD and DVD library

a sound system

lounge

kitchen

store room

toilets

computer room

toilets

sports hall

basketball court

tennis court

* What is it in your language? Find out!

Carnivals and fetes

How do the British have fun in the summer? One way is go to a carnival or a fete. Carnivals take place in streets all over the country. Summer fetes take place outside in a large space. Everyone hopes for a sunny day! Reorder the words to make the questions in this interview.

Summer fetes

1 live where you do? ....
I live in a village in Yorkshire in the North of England.

2 the what summer happens in? ....
Our school has a summer fete every year. All the family comes. My mum always makes a cake for the **cake competition*** but she never wins!

3 at do what like you best fete the? ....
I like the games. One is called **Throw the sponge***. The teachers put their heads through a hole and we all throw wet sponges at them. It's funny! And there are lots of silly races. My brother loves the **egg and spoon race**. Me and my friends are too old for that. But my dad always runs in the race! Embarrassing*!

4 like was fete last what the? ....
Oh, it was fantastic. An actress from my favourite TV programme opened the fete. She's really good-looking*! I got her autograph*.

5 buy did anything you? ....
Yes, at the **White Elephant stall**. I bought a 1970s Space Invaders game – it's really great!

6 food about what the? ....
There was a really good **barbecue**, with burgers and sausages. And they sold lots of cakes too. Yum!

7 win you anything did? ....
No, but my girlfriend, Danielle, was really lucky, She bought a **tombola** ticket and won a huge box of chocolates. And she won a coconut, too.

Use the words in bold as captions for these pictures.

....

....

....

....

....

....

Carnival time

Think about a street carnival you know about. Answer these questions.

1 When is the carnival?
2 What do people wear?
3 What do people eat?
4 What do people do?

Angela answered some questions about her town. Match the questions and answers.

1 Where do you live? ....
2 What happens in the summer? ....
3 What happens on the day? ....
4 What are the costumes like? ....
5 What was the theme last year? ....
6 Who was the Carnival Queen? ....
7 Is there anything to eat? ....
8 What's your favourite thing? ....

a The carnival starts in the afternoon. There's a procession* with floats*. They drive really slowly down the street. There's lots of music and dancing, and people do really silly things.

b Actually it was me! I wore a beautiful dress and a crown*. I had to sit on a throne* on a float and wave at people.

c Well, we have a street carnival here with beautiful floats – floats are decorated* lorries. Each year there's a theme and each team decorates a float and makes costumes. The best float wins a prize.

d I live in Somerset in the south-west of England.

e Yeah, hot dogs and burgers – and candy floss*!

f The music. It's so loud – it's great! And there are lots of live bands, too.

g They're really beautiful. People spend months making them. Some of them are crazy!

h Ancient Egypt. It was fun. My mum's office did Tutankhamen's tomb.

What are the differences and similarities with other carnivals you know?

Can you guess what the theme is for each costume?

> Star Wars   Pirates   Ghosts
> Wild West   Tropical Island

1 ....
2 ....
3 ....
4 ....
5 ....

*What is it in your language? Find out!

Music and theatre festivals

Festivals

Where are the best places to go for music, theatre and fun? Where are the hip* places to be every summer? Here are our readers' recommendations* of their top festival hot spots.

A The Glastonbury Festival

This is the biggest music festival in Britain and it happens on a farm in the west of England! The first festival was in 1970 with only 1,500 people! Now about 140,000 people come and you can see famous acts like REM, Coldplay and Robbie Williams. There's a theatre, a cabaret*, a circus, a cinema and loads of stalls* selling clothes and food, too. It's enormous! I always camp. If it rains, it gets really muddy* – but that's part of the fun! The money goes to charities* like Greenpeace and Oxfam. You have a fantastic time – and you help the world, too!
Alex

B The Edinburgh Festival

The Edinburgh Festival is the coolest event in the world! It's in August and lasts for five weeks. In fact, there are two festivals – the official* one with lots of plays, ballet, opera and stuff and the unofficial* Fringe Festival. The Fringe is bigger than the official festival and there are more unusual* plays and comedy. The Fringe sells over a million tickets every year! Nearly every pub, bar and street corner has a show! I love the comedy* shows. They're really funny. The festival ends with an incredible firework display.
Jamie

C The WOMAD Festival

WOMAD stands for the World of Music, Arts and Dance. Every year, the world comes to Reading! You can see performers* from different countries and cultures. You can listen to music from Ireland and Thailand, dance to African drummers* and learn how to make Brazilian masks*. You can chill out* to the music of Tibet or go to a reggae gig*. There are different kinds of food to eat and ethnic* things to buy. You meet people from other countries. Last year, I met a boy from Spain. Now I'm studying Spanish!
Tina

D Reading Festival

This is the oldest rock festival in Britain – and the best! It started in 1960 when it was called the Jazz and Blues festival. In the 1960s, there were also bands such as The Rolling Stones and The Who. I love the Reading Festival because all my favourite bands and singers play here – Blur, Eminem, Oasis, Red Hot Chilli Peppers, Marilyn Manson. It's so cool. And it's big, too. People eat more than a quarter of a million burgers and hot dogs in three days! Can you believe it?
Baz

Read about the festivals and find the answers to these questions.

1 Which is the oldest rock festival?
2 At which two festivals can you go to the theatre?
3 Where can you see lots of plays?
4 Which festival has mostly ethnic music?

5 Which two cities have two festivals?
6 Which festival takes place on a farm?
7 Which festival changed its name?
8 Where do you give money to charity?

Which festival would you like to go to? Have you ever been to a pop, theatre or film festival?

Find the names of singers and bands in the word square.

1 M _ _ _ _ _ _ A _ _ _ _

2 R _ _ _ _ _ W _ _ _ _ _ _

3 M _ _ _ _ _ _ _ _

4 A _ _ _ _ _ K _ _ _ _ _

5 D _ _ _ _ B _ _ _ _

6 W _ _ _ _ _ _ _

7 C _ _ _ _ _ _ _

8 T _ _ D _ _ _ _ _ _ _

9 R _ _ _ _ _ _ _ _

10 F _ _ _ _ _ S _ _ _

11 S _ _ _ _ _ _ _ _

12 P _ _ _ C _ _ _ _ _ _

13 P _ _ _

14 S _ S _ _ _ _ C _ _ _

15 B _ _ _

16 B _ _ _ _ _

17 O _ _ _ _

18 I _ _ _ M _ _ _ _ _

19 M _ D _ _ _ _ _ _

H	O	P	P	H	I	L	C	O	L	L	I	N	S	U	S
B	I	V	U	E	D	N	O	A	L	U	A	P	A	E	K
L	C	O	L	R	T	I	L	S	O	I	T	K	B	I	J
U	B	R	P	O	L	A	D	I	F	J	O	W	F	R	A
E	I	H	J	B	A	P	P	S	A	M	M	I	A	O	N
W	W	A	G	B	S	A	L	N	Z	S	I	F	T	N	S
M	A	S	S	I	V	E	A	T	T	A	C	K	B	M	U
O	M	E	U	E	V	R	Y	G	U	M	K	L	O	A	G
T	T	R	E	W	O	B	M	E	R	T	I	N	Y	I	A
O	D	A	V	I	D	B	O	W	I	E	T	S	S	D	B
R	J	D	F	L	I	F	C	E	B	A	T	F	L	E	A
H	T	I	R	L	E	R	Z	E	G	P	E	A	I	N	B
E	M	O	D	I	R	V	E	A	P	W	N	K	M	U	E
A	X	H	I	A	T	H	E	D	A	R	K	N	E	S	S
D	H	E	L	M	S	O	S	O	L	I	D	C	R	E	W
S	E	A	M	S	D	Y	N	A	M	I	T	E	F	T	O
D	R	D	R	R	L	O	T	X	Y	B	U	S	T	E	D
F	H	O	W	E	S	T	L	I	F	E	Q	U	F	V	Y

Robbie Williams

Sugababes

Fatboy Slim

Ms Dynamite

*What is it in your language? Find out!

Let's dance!

Whether you prefer breakdancing, morris dancing, salsa or disco, dancing is a great way to keep fit and to meet people. Read the interview below and write the type of dancing next to the pictures.

Do you want to dance? Well, get out your bells, ribbons*, hankies* and flowers, and let's go ... morris dancing!

2 ....

1 ....

3 ....

Why do I need all those things?
They are the traditional decorations* of morris dancers. They add them to their clothes to make them look more colourful – and to make a noise.

That doesn't sound very modern.
Morris dancing is at least five hundred years old. Some people believe it comes from Spain. Others think it comes from ancient Celtic traditions.

But what is morris dancing?
Well, it isn't as easy as disco dancing. People practise together regularly*. Morris dancing involves jumping and hitting sticks* with other dancers.

Do many young people do it?
Well ..., no. It's a minority* interest. A more popular dance with younger people is salsa!

But that isn't British!
Of course not, but the UK has lots of people who love dancing salsa. It's hip* to salsa!

It's a Latin American dance, isn't it?
That's right. It's fun, easy to learn and a good way to keep fit. And maybe the best thing is ... you need a partner, so it's a great way to make friends. But if that isn't your taste, don't forget breakdancing.

Great! Hip-hop's my favourite music. The only problem is ... I don't know how to do it.
Don't worry. There are dance classes all over the UK. But you have to be fit!

Fit?
Breakdancing is like a mix of athletics and acrobatics. You need to be strong and have a good sense of balance*. Breakdancers spend a lot of time with their heads or hands on the ground. And they do a lot of spinning* on their knees, neck, hands, elbows and head! You can get hurt, so you have to be careful.

Mmmm. That sounds difficult. Maybe I'll learn morris dancing!

Which dance ...

1 can be dangerous? ....

2 uses a lot of objects? ....

3 may come from Spain? ....

4 is danced to rap? ....

5 is good for making friends? ....

6 is traditional in Britain? ....

7 is danced with a partner? ....

8 involves* parts of the body touching the floor?
....

Want to party? Why not go to a Ceilidh?

A Ceilidh (pronounced 'kaylie') is a Gaelic word, the native language of Scotland and Ireland. It was originally an informal* meeting of people with folk music, singing, dancing and story-telling. In the old days in Ireland and Scotland, people used to meet in cottages and pass the time with music and song.

Today, it's a party for people of all ages with folk* dancing and a traditional band. The instruments might include a violin, a squeezebox, a guitar, a harmonica, a bhodran and a piano. You have to learn the dance moves. But don't worry, there is always a 'caller'. He tells you what to do!

What are these instruments? Write their names in the crossword.

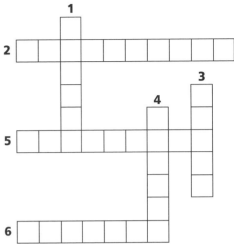

Learn a ceilidh dance!

The Circassian Circle
1 Men and women form a circle and hold hands.
2 All dancers advance four steps.
3 All dancers go back four steps.
4 Women advance four steps and clap hands.
5 Women go back four steps.
6 Men advance four steps and clap hands,
7 Men turn clockwise* and move to the woman who was on their left.
8 All dancers spin* with their new partners.
9 Partners cross hands (right to right and left to left).
10 All dancers walk anti-clockwise* around the room.

Now start again!

Now you try and perform the dance!

*What is it in your language? Find out!**

The High Street

Most teenagers love shopping and the High Street is a good place to look for clothes, music and magazines or to meet friends for a coffee or a snack. Can you label these clothes and accessories*?

trousers
T-shirt
sweatshirt
coat
jacket
skirt
shirt
belt
boots
cap

1 ....
2 ....
3 ....
4 ....
5 ....
6 ....
7 ....
8 ....
9 ....
10 ....

Which shops is Janine calling from?

1 ❝ I'm listening to some great music. I think I'll buy it. ❞

2 ❝ I want to buy some sun cream for my holiday. ❞

3 ❝ I'm having a nice coffee. I'm going to go home soon. ❞

4 ❝ I'm looking at some magazines. I don't think I'll buy one today. ❞

5 ❝ I don't know which one to buy. The detective* story or the love story. ❞

6 ❝ I'm in Bond Street. There's a bit of a queue*. I only want some stamps. ❞

7 ❝ I'm trying on this really brilliant second-hand* 1960's jacket. ❞

8 ❝ I'm in Bond Street. Yum – that's delicious. ❞

KEY:
a post office
b newsagent's
c bakery
d bookshop
e chemist's
f clothes shop
g shoe shop
h music shop
i stationer's
j charity shop
k department store
l electrical store
m café

BOND STREET

QUEEN ROAD

NEW STREET

Call your partner and tell them what you're doing. Your partner has to guess where you are.

Let's go shopping in the High Street.
Can you sort out these dialogues? Rewrite them on the lines.

The shoe shop

I'm afraid they're too small.

Of course. What size are you?

Just a moment. Here you are.

Size 7.

Yes. These are much better, thanks.

OK, would you like to try a bigger size?

I'd like to try on these trainers, please.

Reorganise the dialogue.

....

....

....

....

....

....

....

The bookshop

like hi buy to book I'd this

£5.99 be that'll

you are here

much very thanks

you would like bag a

thanks no

Rearrange the sentences.

....

....

....

....

....

....

The chemist's

Can I .... you?

Yes, I'm .... for a red lipstick.

.... one's nice.

How .... is it?

.... 's £10.99.

Oh, ... you got a cheaper .... ?

This one's nice and it's .... £5.99.

Thanks.

Complete the gaps.

It	much	have	This
only	looking	one	help

The newsagent's

cna I vhea a ehopn adcr, selpae?

hihwc radc lowud ouy ilek?

a £10 neo, sleepa.

rehe oyu rae.

kahnts.

Solve the anagrams.

....

....

....

....

....

Now you try. Go to different shops. Work with a partner and take turns to be the shop assistant and the customer.

*What is it in your language? Find out!

Teen shopping

**British teenagers do part-time* jobs and get pocket money from their parents.
They have a lot of spending power*! So what are they buying?**

Teenage shopping list

1 clothes and accessories

2 toiletries

3 cosmetics

4 sweets and snacks

5 mobile phone cards and ring tones

6 CDs and downloaded* music

7 DVDs

8 computer games

9 books and magazines

10 stationery

What are these teenagers buying in the shops? Look at the list above and write the number.

Gareth ....
I've got some shampoo and shaving cream.

Will ....
I've got some pens and a notebook for school. How boring!

Kerry ....
I've got the latest Harry Potter novel.

Martin ....
I've got a pair of designer* trainers.

Tamsin ....
I've got some crisps and a bar of chocolate! I'm hungry!

Anna ....
I've got some eye make-up and a new lipstick.

What do you buy?

Hi, my family are coming to the UK. I'd like to know what's trendy. What chain stores* do you shop at? What's cool to wear?
Britney ♥

New Look

I like this shop. It's really trendy*. It's got clothes that you see in magazines and they're quite cheap. The last thing I bought here was a pair of trousers.
Abigail

JD Sports

I like skateboarding and windsurfing and JD Sports has a good choice. Their trainers and clothes are great, but they are a bit expensive sometimes. That's the problem with designer clothes! ☹ ☹
Mike

Top Shop

This is an amazing store. The one in Oxford Street in London is huge! And you sometimes see famous people buying clothes here! I like their range* of 60's and 70's clothes. I bought a really cool coat there.
Jessica ☺

The Gap

This is a really good shop. It has great jeans and tops. The only problem is the changing rooms. There's always a queue.
Ashley

Borders

It's a bookshop and a CD store. It's cool because you can listen to any CD in the shop. There are lots of places to sit and read books. There's a café, too. I often hang out* here with my friends!
Christopher

HMV

This is my favourite shop. I go with my friends. They have the latest music, and a huge collection of DVDS. And there's a great computer games department.
Jacob

Lush

The shop smells so good when you go in! And I really like the products*. They're all natural*. They all have such cool names, too. I like the soap best.
Lizzie ☺ ☺

TK Max

I love going to this discount* store. It's huge – you shop with a trolley*! You never know what you are going to find. If you're lucky you can get designer clothes really cheaply. That's the fun of going there.
Sabrina ♥ ♥

Where would you go to ...

1 buy 60s-style clothes? ....

2 buy the latest chart music and computer games? ....

3 find a designer outfit at a good price? ....

4 buy great jeans? ....

5 buy some nice-smelling toiletries? ....

6 choose some sports clothes? ....

7 buy the clothes you see in magazines? ....

8 buy CDs and books? ....

Which of these stores would you like to visit? Why?
Are there chain stores in your country? Which stores are your favourites?

*What is it in your language? Find out!

Bargain-hunting

1 Car boot* sales

All over Britain every weekend there are car boot sales. People arrive in their cars and sell the things they don't want any more: books, CDs, videos, toys, kitchen equipment* and ornaments*. You can find anything if you look! It's great fun and lots of people buy things. Nothing costs very much – 50p or £1, and you can always try and get a better price! Families often use car boot sales to throw old things away.

3 Markets

Many towns have a market day. And you can get lots of bargains*. There are cheap clothes, bags, jewellery and make-up. Usually there are stalls* selling ethnic* clothes, candles and ornaments. Portobello Road in London has a brilliant market on Saturday where you can find lots of vintage* clothes.

2 Charity* shops

Go down any British High Street and you can find lots of charity shops. Many of the people who work in charity shops are volunteers*. The money you spend goes to help the charity. A lot of people buy second-hand* clothes and jewellery. They're cheaper than new and it's fun looking for vintage clothes.

4 Sales

Many teenagers wait for the sales. All the chain stores cut the prices of their clothes at the end of the season. The best sales are at New Year. The TV has advertisements* over Christmas so everyone knows when the sales start. The best sales are very crowded* and it can be tiring! Some people queue over night outside big stores to get the best bargains.

Match the types of shopping with the definitions.

1 when shops and stores offer their goods at reduced prices ....

2 they sell second-hand clothes and goods to help people ....

3 people sell things they don't want any more from the back of their cars ....

4 they are like shops but they sell goods in the open air on a special day ....

What would you try to sell at a car boot sale? Write a description of three things on a piece of paper. Decide on a price for each one. Try to sell them to your partner!

Are you old enough to shop? Let's find out about the legal ages in the UK!

At 12 you can ...
- buy videos and computer games suitable for your age

At 13 you can ...
- ....

At 14 you can ...
- ....

At 15 you can ...
- buy videos and computer games suitable for your age

At 16 you can ...
- buy cigarettes or tobacco
- buy petrol
- buy videos and computer games suitable for your age
- buy liqueur* chocolates
- ....
- ....

At 17 you can ...
- buy an air rifle
- ....
- ....

At 18 you can ...
- buy alcohol
- buy a house
- buy any videos and computer games
- ....
- ....

What about these things? At what age do you think you can do them? Write them in the correct age categories. Check your ideas at the bottom of the page.

buy a motorbike	buy a pet	get a tattoo
buy lottery tickets	buy fireworks	buy a knife
go into a pub but you can't buy alcohol	buy a car	

What are the age limits for these or similar activities in your country?

Answers: 13: buy a pet; 14: go into a pub but you can't buy alcohol; 16: buy lottery tickets, buy a knife; 17: buy a motorbike, buy a car; 18: buy fireworks, get a tattoo

*What is it in your language? Find out!

Pocket money

Most British parents give their teenagers pocket money. Teenagers get between £7 and £20 a week. They spend it on fast food, designer* clothes, the cinema, concerts, magazines and mobile phones.

1 Lazy parents?
37% of parents pay teenagers to clean the lounge.
66% of parents pay teenagers to take the rubbish out.
33% of teenagers have to lay the table, but most parents don't pay for this.

2 Lazy teens?
51% of teenagers don't make their beds before they leave home.
Only 13% of teenagers wash the car for money.
Some parents even pay their teenagers to do their homework.

3 Equality? Not yet!
Boys get more money than girls for most odd jobs.
For washing the dishes, boys get about £4 and girls get about £1.
For cleaning a pet's cage, boys get about £3 and girls get about £1.

4 And if you need some more money?
Teens get an extra £250 a year out of their parents on top of pocket money!
About 50% of teens get gifts* of money from their grandparents.
Go to Mum if you need extra money! She gives more than Dad.

5 Where you live makes a difference!
Parents in Scotland and the North of England give most pocket money.

6 Spending
51% spend their money on clothes.
39% buy cosmetics*, jewellery and toiletries*.
Less than 50% of teenagers save any money.

Match the pictures below with the sections above.

What's it like in your country? What's the same? What's different?

Parents say that over 50% of teenagers are happy to help, but 25% don't want to!
How do teens help in the home? And how much do their parents have to pay them?

How much?!	Average pay for odd jobs
hoovering* the lounge	£1.50
taking the rubbish out	£1.30
washing the car	£2.30
helping to clean the house	£2.75
laying* and clearing* the table	55p
loading* and unloading* the dishwasher	£2.50
cleaning the pet's cage	£1.90
making the bed	75p

This is Bryan Average's list of things to do. How much does he get in one week?
He wants to buy an MP3 player that costs £200. How long does he have to save for?

Bryan's jobs

Take the rubbish out once a week
Load and unload the dishwasher on
Monday, Wednesday and Friday
Make your bed every day except Sunday
Help to clean the house on Saturday
Clean Pete the parrot's cage once a week
Hoover the lounge once a week
Wash the car once a week

We asked some teenagers to tell us about their pocket money.

I get £35 a month. I have to take the rubbish out and tidy my room.
Emma, 15, Edinburgh

I get £10 a week. But I have to clean the car, hoover the house and load and unload the dishwasher. I usually save the money.
James, 12, Sheffield

I get £7.50 a week. I have to be 'good' but I don't have to do any jobs for the money.
Iain, 13, Cardiff

I get £5 a week. But our neighbours* go away a lot and they give me £25 a week for looking after their cats.
Richard, 13, Belfast

I get £15 a week if I keep my room tidy. If I help my mum round the house, I get more money.
Lina, 14, Exeter

I get £80 a month. I know that's generous*. I have to pay for clothes and cosmetics and phone cards. I help to clean the house and tidy my room.
Samirah, 16, Bedford

Who ...

1 probably gets the most money? ....

2 probably gets the least money? ....

3 probably does the most work? ....

4 helps the neighbours? ....

5 doesn't have to do any jobs? ....

6 gets more if they help more? ....

*What is it in your language? Find out!

Part-time jobs

Many teenagers in Britain do part-time jobs to earn more money. But there are laws about how long young people can work and what sort of jobs they can do. Read the information and decide which jobs these teenagers do.

> babysitter   shelf stacker   paper boy   cook   shop assistant

JOB:
1 ....
Wednesday
I've got a new job. I work at the supermarket. I hate it. I work three evenings a week, from six to ten. I have to put products* on the shelves*. The staff aren't allowed to have a chat except in the breaks. [   ] I earn £4 an hour, which is OK. But it's hard doing my homework before I go out to work.

JOB:
2 ....
Friday
I'm so tired. I've worked three evenings this week in the local fast food restaurant. I come home and have a shower before I go to bed because my clothes smell of grease*. My job is to cook the burgers and chips. All evening! We have to wear a special uniform which I hate too. I get paid badly, but I do it so I can go out with my mates.[   ] It must be better than making the food.

JOB:
3 ....
Tuesday
Hi, there. I'm back from my paper round. I'm exhausted*. I do this five times a week. I get up at 6.00 am. I have to get to the paper shop early to get the newspapers. I always deliver to the same streets so I know which house has which paper. [   ] Why do people want to read more on a Sunday? I earn £25 a week – the money's useful*. I have to go now and get ready for school. That's right! I do this before school!

JOB:
4 ....
Saturday
Hi! I'm writing this at 11 o'clock at night. I do babysitting, and I've just got back! I love children – I like playing with them. [   ] Once they're in bed, I can watch TV. This evening I did my homework. The family I babysit for left me a pizza and a cola. They brought me home too. I get £3.50 an hour for babysitting – I think it's good money. I'm saving for a new computer.

JOB:
5 ....
Saturday
Well, it's 7.00 a.m. and I have ten minutes before I leave! I work in a computer shop. I do it because I know a lot about IT. I like helping the customers, even the rude ones! I get extra money if I sell a computer, which is brilliant. Yesterday I sold a laptop* to this guy*. [   ] I never get bored. Well, I'm working with computers – and I love them. I'd like to work here when I leave school.

Where do these sentences come from?
a But I don't like getting them to bed!
b I'd like to serve* the food.
c Then I can have a laugh with my mates.
d On Sundays the papers have extra sections* and they are really heavy.
e He bought a printer too.

Money management

How much do you spend in an average* week? Are you good at controlling your money?
Do you manage to save any money? Look at what these teenagers spend each week and
answer the questions.

Who ...

1 spends most on going out with friends? ....

2 spends a lot of money phoning people? ....

3 goes to the cinema regularly*? ....

4 buys music? ....

5 saves most? ....

6 has an unusual* pet? ....

7 likes fashion? ....

8 plays computer games? ....

Money planner

OUTGOINGS*	AVERAGE PER WEEK			
	Ahmed	**Lucy**	**Chris**	**Melissa**
Going out with friends	£4	£8		£5
Food and drink	£3		£3	
Cosmetics and make-up		£2		£2
CDs			£4	
DVDs				
Cinema tickets	£4	£2		
Computer games		£3		
Other	£4 (phone cards)		£3 (food for pet snake)	£8 (clothes)
Total outgoings	£15	£15	£10	£15
Total income* from pocket money, gifts, jobs	£20	£15	£12	£22
Any left to save?	£5	No!	£2	£7

What about you? Fill in the money planner and find out!

Money planner

OUTGOINGS	AVERAGE PER WEEK
Going out with friends	
Food and drink	
Cosmetics and make-up	
CDs	
DVDs	
Cinema tickets	
Computer games	
Other	
Total outgoings	
Total income from pocket money, gifts, jobs	
Any left to save?	

*What is it in your language? Find out!

Work experience

From the age of 15, 90% of British students experience what work is like by having a job placement with a company. They work up to 40 hours a week. Students don't get paid – but they learn what full-time work is really like! They write a report for their school. They sometimes keep a personal diary, too.

Read Max's report and answer the questions.

1 In which company was his work experience? ....

2 What sort of jobs did he do? ....

3 What was Ms Prentice like? ....

4 Did Max enjoy his work experience? ....

My work experience

I spent a very interesting week at Bainbridge Publishing. My supervisor* was called Ms Prentice and she was always very helpful and gave me lots of useful advice*. I did jobs like photocopying, filing* and checking documents. I enjoyed this and time seemed to pass very quickly.
I soon learned the importance of being on time. I don't think I had any bad experiences* or made any big mistakes. I liked my colleagues* a lot and we often chatted about fascinating things. I just want to say that I think Ms Prentice was really nice and I hope she reads this. Max

Now read Max's diary. How many differences can you find?

Monday

I am SO tired. It's really boring. I'm doing things like filing, checking letters and things for mistakes and photocopying. My desk is in a corner. That's good. It means I can sleep sometimes! Ms Prentice my supervisor is a bit weird*!

Tuesday

I got in late. Ms Prentice wasn't very happy. All the people here are really unfriendly. They don't talk. They don't smile. All they do is look at the stupid computers all day and drink tea and coffee. I had a can of cola – and I spilled it all over my keyboard*. Big mistake! They had to give me a new one.

Wednesday

I had to do loads of photocopying today. There were 2,000 pages. And I photocopied the wrong stuff! Ms Prentice went really red! I have to do them all again tomorrow.

Thursday

Only ten minutes late. I can't keep my eyes open. I've got to do all that photocopying! But I can do it tomorrow. I've been surfing the Internet* most of today. I bought some CDs online* and I checked out some cool websites*.

Friday

Big trouble! I arrived at a quarter to ten and Ms Prentice wanted the photocopies at nine o'clock! I hadn't done them. Then she discovered* all the websites I'd visited yesterday. And then she found my diary. That's right. I wrote this at work. I have to see her in five minutes. I think I have to apologise*!

What things did Max do wrong?
What do you think is the worst thing he did?

Jobs word search

Unscramble the anagrams and find the jobs in the word search.

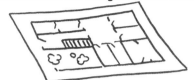

1 TETRAICHC

2 RDREARHIESS

3 YARTCRESRE

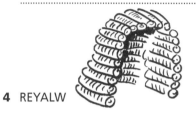

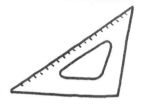

4 REYALW

5 ENEINREG

6 SANIUTOLJR

7 ELCPIO FECOIFR

8 HFEC

9 REAELCN

10 EARTWI

11 TCRAO

12 RAFRME

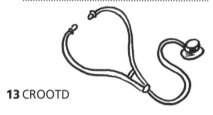

13 CROOTD

14 CEAETRH

15 PSOH ATSNTSAIS

A	R	C	H	I	T	E	C	T	C	O	L	P	I	N	J
B	I	V	U	E	D	N	O	E	A	C	T	O	R	S	O
H	C	S	L	R	T	G	L	A	O	I	T	L	B	H	U
A	B	R	E	O	L	I	D	C	F	C	O	I	J	O	R
I	I	H	J	C	A	N	P	H	A	M	H	C	A	P	N
R	F	A	G	B	R	E	L	E	Z	S	I	E	T	A	A
D	A	A	S	I	V	E	A	R	T	A	C	O	F	S	L
R	M	E	R	E	V	R	T	G	U	M	K	F	B	S	I
E	T	R	E	M	O	B	M	A	R	T	I	F	Y	I	S
S	D	A	C	L	E	A	N	E	R	E	T	I	G	S	T
S	J	D	F	L	I	R	C	E	B	Y	T	C	L	T	A
E	T	I	D	O	C	T	O	R	G	P	E	E	X	A	B
R	M	O	D	I	R	V	E	A	P	W	N	R	M	N	E
L	A	W	Y	E	R	H	E	W	A	I	T	E	R	T	J

What job would you like to do when you leave school?

*What is it in your language? Find out!

School rules

Every school has its rules. But what do these British students think about them? Let's find out!

We have to arrive at school on time. We have to get to all our classes on time. It's a problem for me because I don't wear a watch! And we mustn't run along the corridors*. *Asma*

In the computer room we can use the Internet, but the teachers check the sites* we visit. And we mustn't go onto a chat room*. But that's a good rule, I think. *Tracey*

We mustn't wear make-up. We mustn't chew* gum. And we mustn't listen to our iPods. That's terrible! *Sara*

We have to stand up when the teacher enters the room. We have to wear a uniform – a blazer* and a tie. And we have to do two hours' homework every evening. We mustn't go out of the school gates at lunchtime. *Nick*

We don't have to wear a school uniform at my school. We just have to wear smart clothes – a sweater, trousers, shoes – we mustn't wear jeans or trainers. *Jonathan*

We can only use mobile phones during breaks and at lunchtime. We mustn't use them during lessons. Some of my mates send text messages during exams! It's wrong, but it's difficult for teachers to stop it. *Jamie*

Look at the pictures and say what they are doing wrong.

What must students do? What mustn't they do?
Write the school rules.

wear   use   run   do   listen   chew   arrive   smoke

YOU MUST FOLLOW THE RULES

1 ....

2 ....

3 ....

4 ....

5 ....

6 ....

7 ....

8 ....

Do you have the same school rules in your school?
Invent some rules for your ideal school.

SCHOOL RULES	
Must	**Mustn't**

School subjects

**Students in British schools study a lot of different subjects.
Read on to find out what they study.**

Find the school subjects by matching the two halves.
Write the subjects here.

....

....

....

....

....

....

....

....

....

....

Foreign Lan | **ience** | **tory** | **His**

Eng | **sic** | **lish** | **t**

Geog | **Scie** | **Physical Edu** | **ths** (× 30=)

Mu | **raphy** | **cation** | **ma** | **Bio** | **Ma** (525 / 25)

Dra | **Ar** | **logy** | **guages** | **Computer Sc** | **nce**

Jane has to go shopping before the new school term. What is she studying. Write the subjects.

1 She has to buy paints and a sketch* book.   ....

2 She has to have a calculator*.   ....

3 She needs a new atlas*.   ....

4 She has to buy a violin.   ....

5 She needs a new tracksuit and trainers.   ....

6 She needs to update* her software*.   ....

Barry never finished his timetable. Can you complete it for him?

1 He doesn't do Geography on Tuesday, Wednesday or Friday.
2 He does English every day except Friday.
3 He has three Art lessons a week. At the
   end of the week he has a double lesson
4 He does Drama after Maths one morning.
5 He does P.E. in the morning before Geography.
6 He does French on the same day as double Science.
7 He does Computer Science on the same
   day as Drama.

> Geography   French   Drama
> Computer Science   P.E.   Art   English

	Monday	Tuesday	Wednesday	Thursday	Friday
1	English	English	Maths		P.S.E.[1]
2	Maths			Geography	DT[2]
3	French	P.E.	Art		
4	Science	Science	English	Maths	
5		Science		History	Maths

Which subjects do you study in your school?
What's your favourite subject? Why?
What's your least favourite subject? Why?

Glossary: [1]PSE – Personal and Social Education: This includes discussions about things that concern teenagers, including relationships and personal health. [2]DT – Design and Technology: This includes technical drawing, metal work and wood work.

Students talk about their favourite teachers. But what do they teach?

Mrs Jamieson's really interesting. She's visited lots of
different countries, so she makes the subject come alive.   ....

Mr Allen's got a good accent*. His wife is from Paris, so that helps!   ....

I'm not very good at working with numbers.
But Ms Magrane is really nice and patient.   ....

Mr Clarke's very funny. He tells jokes and helps us to relax.
We play games as well. You can feel a bit nervous*
when you have to act, so it's really good.   ....

Mr Hall used to be a professional footballer. He's really enthusiastic*!   ....

* What is it in your language? Find out!

The school system

What do you know about the British school system? When do students start at primary school? When do they go to secondary school? Look at the information and complete the table.

> The majority* of students receive free education in state schools. However, 7% of students attend private schools.

> You have to stay at school until you're sixteen. But about 70% of students stay on for another 2 years to take A' levels.

> Happy 14th birthday! Sorry you've got maths and science exams this week!

> An increasing number of students are now going on to study at university. Northern Ireland has the highest percentage with 45%, but there are 40% in Scotland and 35% in England and Wales

> Loads of people take a gap year now. That's a year off between school and university. They go travelling or get some work experience. It's a good opportunity* to see the world!

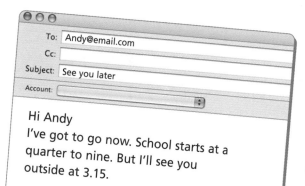

To: Andy@email.com
Cc:
Subject: See you later
Account:

Hi Andy
I've got to go now. School starts at a quarter to nine. But I'll see you outside at 3.15.

Happy birthday and good luck at school.

> I've got quite good qualifications*. I took nine GCSEs when I was sixteen, and I passed all of them. And then, two years later, I got three A levels.

Education factfile

Compulsory education
- Full time education in the UK is compulsory* between the ages of ……… and ……… .

- 93% of pupils receive …………………………… .
- 7% go to …………………………… .

Primary school
- For children between 5 and 11.

Secondary school
- For students of 11 years plus.
- School starts at about …………………………… and finishes at about …………………………… .
- Students take national exams in …………………………… and science at 14.

- Students takes GCSE exams at ……… , AS level exams at 17, and A' levels or Advanced level exams at ……… .

University
- Many students take a ……………… ……………… between school and university.
- Approximately ……………… of young people in England and Wales, ……………… in Scotland and ……………… in Northern Ireland go to university.

Private schools
These are schools where parents pay for their children's education. There are some very famous old private schools (called Public schools) such as Eton and Harrow.

* What is it in your language? Find out!

My day at school

Read Jimmy's diary and number the pictures.

Monday

Today was a bit of a disaster*. I went to bed really late last night because I had to finish my homework. I know, I left it to the last moment. But who wants to do homework at the weekend? Anyway, I was so tired I didn't hear the alarm clock. So Jessica was already in the bathroom and she takes a long time. There wasn't time for breakfast so I said goodbye to Mum and I ran out of the house. But I didn't catch the bus. I missed it by seconds! So I had to walk to school and I got there at half past nine.

Mr Harrison, the science teacher, was horrible. Really horrible. There were three main reasons. One: I was late. Two: I wasn't wearing my tie. And three: I didn't have my homework. I left the house so quickly that I forgot my tie and all my books! I explained exactly what happened but he didn't believe me. Why are teachers so suspicious*?

The rest of the morning was OK. Maths was boring. History was boring. And then it was lunchtime. But I had a problem – I didn't have any lunch. Yes, that's right. I forgot my sandwiches, too. And I didn't have any money to buy a snack. I felt so hungry! My best mate Johnno gave me some chocolate. I ate it really quickly but it wasn't enough.

During the French class, Alison and her friends pointed at me and laughed. I like Alison. I mean, I REALLY like her. She's wonderful. But I don't like people laughing at me. Then the teacher said, 'James, go to the cloakroom and clean your face.' I left the room. When I looked in the cloakroom mirror there was chocolate all over me. I guess I ate the chocolate too quickly.

And then in my English class I fell asleep. I couldn't help it. I was so tired and hungry. So Ms Anderson woke me up and sent me to the headmaster. Mr Blake is a tall big man and he wasn't very happy. In fact, he gave me loads of extra homework.

I got a text message from Alison a few minutes ago. It said, 'Sorry for laughing'. That was nice of her. Did I mention that she's fantastically attractive?

It's ten o'clock now. It's getting late. I think it's time to start my homework.

Who is ...

Johnno? Ms Anderson? Alison? Mr Blake? Mr Harrison? Jessica?

Lunch time

At school, British teenagers can have school dinners, take sandwiches or buy sandwiches at school or from sandwich bars nearby. What do these teenagers have for lunch?

What do you have for lunch?

David

I take a lunch box to school. I make sandwiches, and I take a piece of fruit, a yoghurt* and fruit juice.

Michael

Lisa

I have a packed lunch. Usually it's a baguette*, a packet of crisps, an apple and a chocolate bar.

I like my school dinners. I have chips every day with burgers or pizza and a cola. Excellent!

Nick

I have school lunch. There's a good choice*. I like chicken but I don't like vegetables very much. I hate peas.

Amanda

I buy a sandwich from the school canteen* – my favourite filling* is ham and salad. Mum gives me £2 a day to spend. I sometimes have a cake, too.

I have a packed lunch. I make my own sandwiches. My favourite filling is cheese. And I like tomatoes. I usually take milk to drink and a packet of crisps.

Stephanie   Dan

I preferred* the old school dinners – you know, chips, pizza, burgers. Now they are doing healthier food like meat, vegetables and potatoes. It's OK I suppose and it's better for you!

Mary

I buy a baguette from the local sandwich bar. Sometimes I have a smoothie*, too. I like drinking milk and the fruit is good for you.

**Write one or more names.
Who ...**

1 has school lunch? ....

2 has packed lunch? ....

3 goes out for lunch? ....

4 makes their own sandwiches? ....

5 likes salads? ....

6 has crisps? ....

7 doesn't like vegetables? ....

8 has fruit? ....

9 do you think has the healthiest lunch? ....

10 do you think has the unhealthiest lunch? ....

Alice

I always have a salad in the school canteen. They do really nice things like carrot salad and tuna salad. And I usually drink fruit juice.

**Which lunch do you like best?
What do you have for lunch?**

Circle Sandwich Bar

You'll love our fresh sandwiches and brilliant smoothies*. All of our sandwiches have passed our quality* test!

Circle's favourite sandwiches

Totally tuna	£2.90
Cool chicken	£2.50
Cheeky cheese and tomato	£2.40
Heavenly ham	£2.80
Excellent egg mayonnaise	£2.30
Breakfast bacon	£2.50

Circle drinks

Fun and delicious – try our fruit smoothies!

Brilliant banana smoothie	£1.90
Marvellous mango smoothie	£1.90
Silly strawberry smoothie	£2.20
Charming chocolate smoothie	£2.50
Cola	£1.70
Mineral water	£1.50

Desserts*

'Death by chocolate' cake	£2.20
Funky flapjack*	£1.90
Blueberry muffin*	£2.20

How much? What are the totals for the food and drink?

1

tuna sandwich	£............
mango smoothie	£............
flapjack	£............
Total:	£............

2

chicken sandwich	£............
chocolate smoothie	£............
muffin	£............
Total:	£............

3

egg mayonnaise sandwich	£............
strawberry smoothie	£............
chocolate cake	£............
Total:	£............

4

ham sandwich	£............
mineral water	£............
muffin	£............
Total:	£............

Mike and Emily are at the Sandwich Bar. Can you complete the dialogue?

I'd   much   are   Can   have

Assistant: Hi, guys. What can I get you?

Mike: Can I **(1)**...................... a tuna sandwich and a banana smoothie, please?

Emily: And can I have a cheese and tomato sandwich and a coke, please?

Assistant: Cool. Anything else?

Emily: Mmm. **(2)**...................... like the chocolate cake, please.

Mike: (3)...................... I have a flapjack, please?

Emily: How **(4)**...................... is that?

Assistant: That's £13.30.

Mike: Here you **(5)**...................... .

Work with a partner. You are at the Circle Sandwich Bar. One of you is the assistant and one is the customer. Make a dialogue together.

*What is it in your language? Find out!

British breakfasts

Can you match these favourite British breakfasts with the descriptions?

1 It isn't eaten every day, but it is still a favourite. A full fried breakfast includes egg, bacon, sausage, tomatoes, mushrooms and baked beans.

a Croissants

2 This is a real classic*. Four million bowls of cornflakes are eaten every day! Supermarkets sell lots of varieties.

b English breakfast

3 This French breakfast bread came from Hungary. It is a popular* British breakfast too, and it tastes best eaten warm, served with coffee.

c Scrambled egg

4 Put a slice of bread in the toaster. Wait a minute for it to pop out, and spread it with butter and marmalade!

d Cereal and milk

5 A lot of British people only have a hot drink before they leave home in the morning.

e Bacon sandwich

6 This is a popular breakfast. It's quick and easy and good for you. Britons' favourite is the banana!

f Yoghurt

7 It's good for you, and lots of people eat it for breakfast. They often eat it with fruit or cereal.

g Coffee

8 It's great if you want something savoury*. Grill some bacon, and put it between two slices of bread. About 1.5 million are eaten every day!

h Toast

9 These are beaten* eggs, cooked gently and stirred* at the same time. They should be nice and light.

i Fruit

Take the letters in bold from a–g to find a popular Scottish breakfast cereal
Take the letters in bold from h–i to find what it is made from.

P.. is made from ....s .

This breakfast is a Scottish classic. The cereal is cooked with water or milk and served hot in a bowl. People often add sugar and milk.

What about you?
Do you have breakfast every day?
What do you have for breakfast?
Have you ever eaten any of these breakfasts?
Which of these breakfasts do you think are international?

Comfort food

Comfort food is food that makes you feel happy and relaxed*! It is often a traditional* food. Here are some favourite UK comfort foods.

bangers and mash

Sausages
Five million sausages are eaten every day in the UK. Sausages and mashed* potato is called 'bangers and mash'. Half of British sausages are eaten for an evening meal. And more sausages are cooked on Saturday in England than on any other day! People also like sausage sandwiches and barbecued sausages.

sponge pudding

Puddings*
In the 1690s a French visitor to London wrote, 'Ah, what an excellent thing is an English pudding'. Sponge puddings are steamed* in water in a saucepan. They are like a hot cake and are served with custard*. Other favourite puddings are rice puddings, fruit pies and Christmas puddings. Nowadays families don't have a pudding every day, but it is still a favourite. People often buy ready-made* traditional puddings now.

tea and biscuits

teapot

kettle

Tea and biscuits
165 million cups of tea are drunk each day in the UK! Tea is often served with biscuits and 98% of Brits have it with milk. You'll find two tea-making things in every British kitchen: the kettle, which is used for boiling the water, and the teapot, which is used for making the tea. But nowadays many teenagers don't drink tea and prefer cold drinks.

Yorkshire pudding

roast lunch

Traditional roast lunch
This is usually served at lunchtime on Sunday. It is when families get together. It consists* of roast meat, usually beef, lamb or pork, served with roast potatoes, Yorkshire pudding (a kind of savoury batter*), vegetables and lots of gravy*! It is often followed by a traditional pudding, too! Sunday lunch is a popular meal to eat out at the pub. And students away from home miss it because a roast lunch means family life.

Now decide if these sentences are true (T) or false (F).
1 Five million plates of bangers and mash are eaten each day. ....
2 About 50% of sausages are eaten in the evening. ....
3 People eat more sausages on Saturday than Monday. ....
4 Sponge pudding is served cold with custard. ....
5 People don't often cook steamed puddings now. ....
6 165 million British people drink tea every day. ....
7 British people use a kettle to boil water. ....
8 Roast lunch is served in the evening on Sunday. ....
9 Yorkshire pudding is eaten with roast meat. ....
10 British people like eating Sunday roast in a pub. ....

Would you like these comfort foods? What's the comfort food and drink in your country?

*What is it in your language? Find out!

Did you know?
If you say something 'isn't your cup of tea', it means you don't like it.

Global food

Do you know what these foods are?
Which ones have you eaten? Did you like them?
If you haven't tried them, would you like to?
Do you think any of these foods are disgusting?
Which foods are not in the text below?

chilli

pineapple

snake

duck

coriander

raw fish

coconut

beans

avocado

seaweed

oats

mozzarella cheese

parsley

Where are these dishes from? Read the descriptions.
Then unscramble the words to find the countries of origin

natladih   diani   tilay/het SUA   panaj
nicah   cixome   nidai/tibrani

Pizza

This Italian food first became popular in the USA.
It is now a favourite food in the UK. It is a flat bread
with mozzarella cheese and tomato on top, baked in
the oven. You can buy it in supermarkets or from
fast food restaurants and pizzerias. British people
like unusual toppings*, including pineapple!

Chicken tikka massala

This is now considered Britain's national dish.
It combines an Indian dish, 'Chicken Tikka', with
the British love of gravy*, the 'Massala'. Indian
restaurants serve 23 million portions* every year,
and you can buy chicken Tikka Massala-flavoured*
sandwiches, crisps and even pizza!

Sweet and sour chicken

Chinese restaurants and take-aways* have been
popular in the UK for over 30 years. Britons love
the taste of sweet and sour and are very fond*
of this dish.

Thai green curry

Thai food is now very popular in Britain. There are
lots of Thai restaurants and many people try to make
the food at home. Thai curries are flavoured with
coriander, hot chillis and coconut milk.

Chicken curry

British people enjoy going to an Indian restaurant
or 'curry house'. And they also enjoy making curry at
home with spices or ready-made* sauces, served with
rice. You can also order an Indian take-away or buy
ready-made curry from a supermarket.

Nachos, tortillas, and tacos

People serve Mexican food at parties. Tortilla chips
(corn crisps) or nachos and tacos (flat breads) are
served with Mexican dips*. Some of them are very
hot! Dips include bean paste*, tomato and
guacamole (avocado dip).

Sushi

There are hundreds of sushi bars in Britain and you
can buy sushi in most supermarkets for lunch or
dinner. It consists* of small rice 'fingers' stuffed
with raw fish and wrapped in seaweed.

Time for tea!

The British have drunk tea for 350 years! The first tea came from China and later from India. In the North of England, 'What's for tea?' means 'What's for dinner?' This is because people drank tea with their meal. Why not learn how to make a perfect cup of tea and impress* your British friends!

Tea for two

You need:
a kettle for boiling the water
a teapot big enough for four cups
three teaspoons of tea or three teabags
two tea cups, teaspoons and saucers
a jug of cold milk

Match the instructions with the pictures. Then put them in order.

A Put on a kettle of water to boil.
B Pour the boiling water onto the tea.
C Pour the tea on top of the milk.
D Warm the teapot with hot water, then pour it away.
E Put the lid on the teapot.

F Add sugar to taste.
G Put the tea or tea bags in the pot.
H Let the tea brew* for five minutes.
I Pour a small amount of milk into each cup.

Write instructions for making a drink from your country.

Types of home

Homes are similar* all over the world. People cook, eat and sleep in them. But look at the details and you can discover* things about the way people live – and what makes them different. The British spend a lot of time in their homes, perhaps because the weather is often cold and wet! But they love their gardens too!

Look at the pictures of typical British things. Find the words in the word square.

C	U	R	T	A	I	N	S	O
C	W	B	G	U	B	A	R	E
O	O	F	A	P	S	B	E	K
M	I	C	R	O	W	A	V	E
P	O	X	D	E	Q	R	L	T
U	S	H	E	D	E	B	L	T
T	D	U	N	I	R	E	A	L
E	A	P	E	T	S	C	W	E
R	T	R	A	F	O	U	N	G
C	A	R	P	E	T	E	J	G
L	A	W	N	M	O	W	E	R

1 You boil water in this. You need it for making tea.
K...

2 Half of British homes have an animal.
P...

3 The British buy more ready-made* meals than other European countries and heat* them up at home.
M...

4 Most British gardens have one. People keep garden furniture and picture 9 in them!
S...

5 One of the most popular* ways to eat in summer – if the weather's dry!
B...

6 It's a fact! The British love plants, flowers and their lawns.
G...

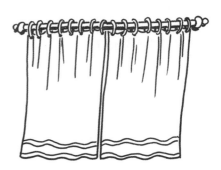

7 In a cold climate* these keep the heat in the room.
C...

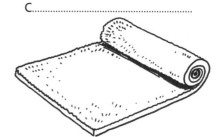

8 This makes the floor warmer.
C...

9 If you love your lawn – you have to cut it!
L...

About half of British homes have one of these. Can you find another word in the word square?

....

*What is it in your language? Find out!

1 ....

2 ....

3 ....

4 ....

6 ....

5 ....

Who lives in which home?

Hi, my name's Jerry. I live in a semi-detached* house in London. We live near a tube* station so it's easy to get around.

Hello, my name's Fatima. I live in a detached* house in York. I'm in a band and we practise in the garage.

Hello, my name's Paul. I live in a bungalow* in Bournemouth. It's OK, but it's difficult to get away from my parents!

Hi, my name's Ellie. I live in a flat in the suburbs* of Edinburgh. I really like dogs but I can't have a pet. It's against the rules.

Hi, my name's Angela. I live in a terraced* house in Dublin. Our house is small and I'm kind of noisy. Our neighbours don't like my music!

Hi, I'm James. I live in a cottage in Wales. Life in the country can be pretty boring. My mum has to drive me to the station.

The UK in numbers

What do you think? Circle the numbers. Check your answers at the bottom of the page.

1 British people watch 10 hours / 15 hours / 25 hours of TV a week.

2 3 million / 7 million / 15 million people own a dog.

3 20% / 50% / 80% of people live in a house.

4 2-3 / 3-4 / 4-5 people live in the average* British home.

5 20% / 50% / 80% of British people regularly* do a sport.

6 30% / 60% / 80% of British homes have a microwave oven.

Answers: 1 25 2 7 3 80 4 2-3 5 50 6 80

What types of homes do people have in your country?

Explore a British home

A typical British house has a small front garden (1) with a gate (2) and a path (3). There is often a porch (4) over the front door (5). There is a larger back garden (6) with a shed (7) in it. The house usually has a loft (8). Some homes have a garage (9) with a drive (10). Can you find these things in the picture?

Where do these things go? Write the numbers in the correct rooms.

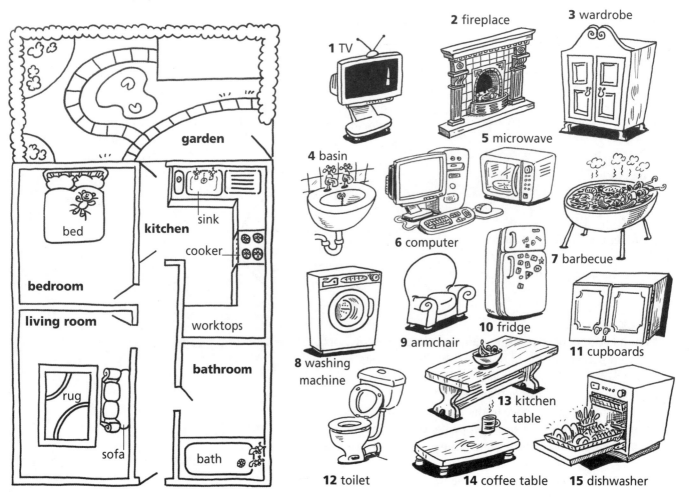

garden

kitchen
sink
cooker
worktops

bed

bedroom

living room

bathroom

rug

sofa

bath

1 TV
2 fireplace
3 wardrobe
4 basin
5 microwave
6 computer
7 barbecue
8 washing machine
9 armchair
10 fridge
11 cupboards
12 toilet
13 kitchen table
14 coffee table
15 dishwasher

Come on a guided tour of a British home! And fill in the gaps while you read!

has	called	love	playing	spend	isn't
use	watch	eat	listen	sit	have

Living room

The centre of British life. People **(1)**........................... TV here, **(2)**........................... to music and often eat their dinners. In fact, people often **(3)**........................... their dinner on a tray* while watching TV. The floor has a carpet so it is comfortable to **(4)**........................... on. Although most houses have central heating*, the fireplace is the focus of the room.

Kitchen

With lots of work surfaces* and appliances*, the British kitchen **(5)**........................... different from other kitchens around the world. But they almost always **(6)**........................... a microwave and an electric kettle. The washing machine is usually in the kitchen too. People sit and chat in the kitchen and there is often a big table.

Read about British homes. What are the similarities and differences with your home?

*What is it in your language? Find out!

Bathroom

Bidets* aren't common in British bathrooms. The toilet is sometimes in a separate room from the bathroom. It's often **(7)**........................... the 'loo'.

Bedroom

Of course, there are the usual things, but one in three British teenagers **(8)**........................... a TV. The typical home is small so many families **(9)**........................... bedrooms for studying and surfing the net*. Teenagers **(10)**........................... a lot of time in their bedrooms and put up posters and photos of their favourite pop stars.

Garden

British people **(11)**........................... their gardens – gardening is a favourite hobby. Teenagers prefer **(12)**........................... football and games on the lawn. And in the summer, families often have barbecues.

British customs

A famous saying is 'When in Rome do what the Romans do'. This means that when you visit a country, you should copy the customs of the people who live there. Imagine you are going to Britain. How well do you know what the British do? Try this quiz and find out.

1 You are introduced to your classmate's friend, Chris. Do you …
a) kiss him on both cheeks?
b) shake* his hand?
c) just say 'How are you?' or 'Hi'?

2 You're a guest at someone's house. You've never been there before. You need to go to the toilet. Do you say …
a) 'Can I use your bathroom?'?
b) 'Where's your toilet, please?'?
c) 'I need to go to the toilet.'?

3 You are invited to your friend's house for dinner. Do you …
a) take nothing – a gift isn't expected*?
b) take a small gift such as a bunch of flowers or a small box of chocolates?
c) take a large present, such as a big box of chocolates, or a cake?

4 You want to buy some stamps in the Post Office. There are some people waiting. Do you …
a) decide where the queue* ends and stand there?
b) go to the window and try to get the attention of the clerk?
c) ask loudly, 'Who is last?' and stand behind them?

5 You have to be at a friend's house at 10 o'clock. You're going on a day trip with his family. Do you …
a) turn up at twenty to ten to show you are keen*?
b) turn up just a few minutes early?
c) turn up at twenty past ten as it's rude to be on time?

6 You accidentally bump* into someone. Do you say …
a) 'Sorry!'?
b) 'Oh, dear!'?
c) 'Pardon!'?

7 You arrive at someone's house. Do you …
a) take off your shoes and walk into the house in your socks?
b) wipe* your shoes well on the mat but keep them on?
c) take off your shoes and put on the slippers your host offers you?

8 You are going to bed. Do you say …
a) 'Goodbye'?
b) 'Good night'?
c) 'Good evening'?

Count up your score and read the results.

| **1 a**1 **b**2 **c**3 | **2 a**3 **b**2 **c**1 | **3 a**1 **b**3 **c**2 | **4 a**3 **b**1 **c**2 |
| **5 a**2 **b**3 **c**1 | **6 a**3 **b**1 **c**1 | **7 a**1 **b**3 **c**1 | **8 a**1 **b**3 **c**1 |

17-24 Wow! Are you sure you aren't British? You will fit in perfectly*!
11-16 Not bad. You may make a few gaffes*, but you won't upset people.
0-10 Oh dear! Every country has its ways of doing things. You need to learn them before you go!

The best answers have a score of 3. Compare these customs with your own country. Which ones are the same or similar? Which ones are different?

Millions of foreign students go to the UK every year to study English, especially in the summer. They often stay with British families (host families). They experience real British family life and learn a lot about the culture.

Read some students' impressions of life in the UK. Match the beginnings and ends of the sentences.

1 I find it difficult to sleep

a the sound of the milkman, but I like the fresh milk on my cereal!

2 The hot and cold water in the bathroom

b they do things after dinner like sport or going to the pub.

3 The family eats early at 6 o'clock, but

c which they heat in the microwave.

4 We eat an amazing variety of food

d comes out of separate taps – the hot water is boiling!

5 My family eats a lot of supermarket dinners,

e they prefer to pick me up by car – it's very kind of them.

6 The dog is allowed to sit on the sofa

f because light comes through the curtains.

7 Some TV channels don't have commercials

g and the cat sleeps on the bed!

8 On Sundays in the town I'm staying in

h so it's great watching a programme without breaks.

9 They don't like me using public transport after dark,

i from all over the world – it's great.

10 In the mornings I get woken up at six o'clock by

j nearly all the shops are open.

Do you think the comments are positive, negative or neutral?
Are any of these things true for your country?

*What is it in your language? Find out!

Cards, cards, cards!

**The British buy more greetings* cards than any other people in the world.
And they send cards for lots of different reasons!**

Write the messages on the cards.

Happy birthday	Love you	Good luck!	Congratulations
Sorry!	Get well soon	Miss you	Thank you

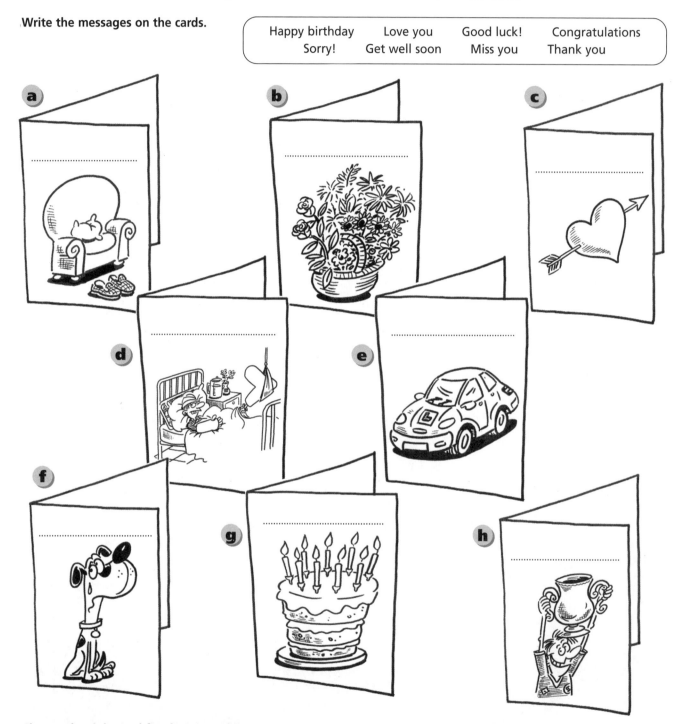

Choose the right card for these people.

1 Rosa has her English test tomorrow. ....

2 Steve has got his exam results* – and they're fantastic! ....

3 You borrowed a DVD from a friend. Oh dear, you can't find it! ....

4 Your best friend is studying in the USA. ....

5 It's your Dad's birthday! ....

6 It's Valentine's Day. Time to send a card to your boyfriend or girlfriend! ....

7 It was your birthday last week. Your got an iPod from your aunt! What an amazing gift! ....

8 One of your friends has got a terrible cold and has to stay at home in bed. ....

Special Days

When is it?
Well, it's any day of the year! You can choose.

Really? So what is it?
It's a very special day. First you choose an activity for your friend or a member* of your family. Then you pay for it. After that you send them a card. The card tells them all about their fantastic day.

What kind of thing can you do?
There are lots of things to choose from. Take a look at the these ideas.

 **7** Go scuba diving in Cornwall

 **1** Go snowboarding!

 **4** Try bunjee jumping

 **8** Learn to cook with chocolate!

 **2** Enjoy a paintballing weekend

 **5** A day at Manchester United

 **9** Have skydiving lessons!

 **3** Learn to play golf!

 **6** Have horse riding lessons

 **10** Go mountain climbing in Scotland

---

Look at the Special Day activities. Which one do you think is …

- the most exciting? ....
- the most frightening? ....
- the most boring? ....
- the most fun? ....

Where are they? Read the speech bubbles and decide.

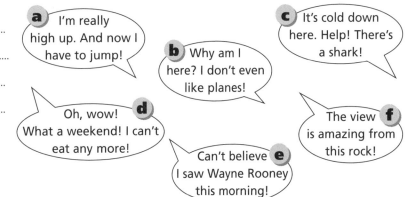

a) I'm really high up. And now I have to jump!

b) Why am I here? I don't even like planes!

c) It's cold down here. Help! There's a shark!

d) Oh, wow! What a weekend! I can't eat any more!

e) Can't believe I saw Wayne Rooney this morning!

f) The view is amazing from this rock!

*What is it in your language? Find out!

Choose a Special Day for your partner.

School proms

**School proms are the latest thing in the UK,
and like many things, they started in the USA.**

Read about prom nights and label the picture with these words.

ball gown	prom king	flowers	theme
prom queen	tuxedo	jewellery	crown

1 ....

2 ....

3 ....

4 ....

5 ....

6 ....

7 ....

8 ....

Prom night is one of the biggest events* of the year in American high schools. At the end of their last year at high school, students go to a huge party. It's great fun. Boys wear tuxedos and girls wear expensive ball gowns and jewellery. Couples traditionally* exchange flowers.

Proms usually have a theme that changes every year. It could be Hollywood or the 1960s … or anything! Students choose the music and the theme.

And proms aren't only fun. They're competitive*, too. Students vote for a Prom King and Queen, a Prince and Princess, and a Duke* and Duchess*.

Read what British teenagers think about prom nights.

> We're going to have a prom this year. I'm really excited. In fact, I've already bought my dress – and the prom is five months away!
> *Maxine*

> It was an amazing experience – probably the best time I've had in my whole life.
> *Charlie*

> I think it's a fantastic idea. I just love parties and dressing up.
> *Amanda*

> I hate the idea of having a party at school. I prefer going to parties at my mates' houses.
> *Jake*

> It was a great way to say goodbye to my school mates. I mean, after school, you often lose touch.
> *Kevin*

> I found it really strange. Everybody looked so different. I mean, boys that were really boring suddenly looked fantastic!
> *Tracey*

Which teenagers have already been to a school prom? ....

Which ones like the idea of a school prom? ....

Do you have school proms in your country? Do you think it's a good idea?

Prom night

It takes months to prepare for 'Prom night'. First, students have to form a committee* because they have to make lots of important decisions. They then decide where to have the prom. (It often isn't at the school). After that, the committee chooses the theme and the music for that year. Next step – they choose the food and drink. Then they arrange the transport. Hired* limousines* are very popular, especially with boys! Then the girls buy or hire their ball gowns and the boys buy or hire their tuxedos. Finally, on the day of the prom, students go to hairdressers, put on their prom outfits and make-up, and wear a smile!

Can you put these pictures of prom preparations in order?

Organise your own class prom.
Put a circle round the best idea – or invent one for yourself.

What venue?

a hotel   a disco   the school gym   other? ....

What theme?

the 1970s   the Titantic   the movies   other? ....

What kind of music?

disco   hip hop   punk   other? ....

What kind of food?

pizzas   Chinese   sandwiches   other? ....

What kind of drink?

fizzy drinks   fruit cocktails   tea and coffee   other? ....

How are you going to arrive?

a helicopter   a limousine   with parents   other? ....

What are you going to take with you?

a handbag   a flower   a mobile phone   other? ....

You can decide these answers!

Who are you going with? ....

Who is going to be the Prom King? ....

Who is going to be the Prom Queen? ....

Yes, I want one to drive 10 people …

*What is it in your language? Find out!

Fireworks in Britain

Britain has a long tradition of fireworks. Here are some of the highlights*!
Read about the history of fireworks in Britain.

Roger Bacon, an English monk*, wrote about his experiments with fireworks in 1242.

Queen Elizabeth I watched the earliest recorded fireworks display* in England at Warwick Castle in 1572. She liked them, and more firework displays followed. The fireworks had a lot of gold and silver explosions*.

The Thames has been a popular location for fireworks for 400 years. The first display was in 1613 for the marriage of King James' daughter. The biggest recent* one was to celebrate the new Millennium in 2000.

There was a huge fireworks display in 1749 over Green Park in London. It took six months to plan, special music was written and a special building (the Temple) was built. It cost £14,500 – a lot of money in those days! Unfortunately, there was an accident and the Temple caught fire!

The Brock family made fireworks in the 19th century. They gave many fantastic displays at Crystal Palace. At the first event, there were over 20,000 people!

The traditional day for fireworks is Guy Fawkes' night on 5th November. Guy Fawkes failed* to blow up the Houses of Parliament. But these days, fireworks are so popular you can see and hear them the whole year!

Now cover the article. Can you remember what these numbers refer to?

1242	1572	1613	20,000
2000	1749	14,500	5th

Two of these facts are false. Can you guess which ones?
Answers at the bottom of the page!

Firework facts

1 Fireworks were invented by the Chinese about 2,000 years ago.
2 Fireworks were introduced to Britain in 1066.
3 Rockets are fast! They can travel at 210 kilometres per hour!
4 Sparklers* are hot! They burn at over 15 times the boiling point of water.
5 There were no coloured fireworks before the 1800s.
6 There's a maximum fine* of £5,000 for throwing a firework in the street.
7 The most popular recent firework is called 'The David Beckham'.
8 39,210 rockets were set off at the same time in Jersey in 1997. That's a world record!

Answers: 2, 7

The Firework Code contains simple safety* instructions. Unfortunately, the words in these instructions have got jumbled. Can you put the words in the right order?

Have fun. Be safe.
Follow the Fireworks Code.

- a in keep fireworks
  .... closed box.
- the follow instructions on
  .... each firework.
- fireworks at all light
  .... arm's length.
- back well stand
  ....
- a firework never back to go
  .... after it has been lit.
- in your fireworks put pocket never
  ....
- throw never fireworks
  ....
- light one sparkler always
  .... at a time.
- children never give sparklers to
  .... under five.
- indoors pets keep
  ....

When's your favourite time for fireworks?
Read the opinions of these British teenagers.

New Year's the best time – at midnight on the last night of the year. It's become a new tradition. It's great.

I like having a firework display on my birthday. It's in February, which is a pretty boring time of the year. Fireworks are a great way to celebrate.

There are huge firework displays for Diwali. That's the Hindu New Year celebration in November. We have candles inside and outside the house, too. It's a festival of lights!

We always set off fireworks when England wins a football match. So we don't have fireworks as often as I'd like!

Guy Fawkes Night's my favourite time. We do all the traditional things. We have a Guy and a bonfire and we eat baked potatoes. Loads of people have firework parties in their gardens. But people have fireworks weeks before 5th November – and weeks afterwards, too!

Did anything surprise you?
When do you have firework displays in your country?

* What is it in your language? Find out!

Answers

pages 6 and 7
ENGLAND

Map of the UK.

Dan's email.

Hi Lisa
Here I am in London. It's the capital of Britain. It's a huge place – **seven (1)** million people live here. That's crowded! The Queen lives in **Buckingham (2)** Palace.
England is really cool. **Birmingham (3)** is amazing. It's got the best night life in **Europe (4)**.
The English are so funny. Many people go to the **beach (5)** for their holidays. There's great **surfing (6)** in Cornwall. But did you know? **Walking (7)** is their favourite outdoor sport! Britain is the **largest (8)** island in Europe. The Channel **Tunnel (9)** goes from England to **France (10)**
See you soon
Dan x

pages 8 and 9
WALES AND SCOTLAND

1e 2f 3b 4d 5a 6c

Jo's emails
1 were went bought (picture b)
2 walked (picture a)
3 see took (picture d)
4 was (picture c)

pages 10 and 11
IRELAND AND NORTHERN IRELAND

Find someone who ...
1 Eileen 2 Liam 3 Cait 4 Jonny 5 Eileen
6 Jonny 7 Eileen 8 Liam 9 Cait 10 Liam

The lucky Irish plant is the
shamrock

pages 12 and 13
MY DUBLIN

Great things to do
1 Go shopping 2 Go to college 3 Eat out
4 See how Guinness is made 5 See how the Vikings lived 6 Go green

Map of Dublin
a 6 b 3 c 5 d 4 e 1 f 2

The Claddagh ring
heart hands crown

pages 14 and 15
BRIGHTON ROCKS!

A The shops **B** The Pavilion **C** The Promenade **D** Sports
E The festival **F** The Palace Pier

Where are Tim and Suzy?
1 Sea Life Centre 2 Brighton Pavilion 3 Promenade
4 Palace Pier (Pleasure Dome) 5 King Alfred Leisure Centre
6 Duke of York's Media Centre 7 The Lanes

Suzy won a teddy bear.
Tim won a computer game.
Anne won an alarm clock.
Adam won a pencil case.

pages 16 and 17
BEATLEMANIA IN LIVERPOOL

1 Thursday 2 Friday 3 Tuesday
4 Wednesday 5 Monday

Crossword

pages 18 and 19
WHAT IS BEING BRITISH?

1 Saquib Donald **2** Saquib **3** Saquib Danielle Donald
4 Saquib Danielle Sam Donald **5** Saquib Sam Donald
6 Saquib Donald **7** Danielle **8** Donald **9** Sam
10 Saquib Sam Donald

Asian Pakistan Punjabi Muslim Bollywood
Chinese Chinatown Chinese New Year
Afro Caribbean black reggae Barbados Bob Marley
White Sunday roast

pages 20 and 21
A MULTICULTURAL MIX

World map
1 North America **2** Europe **3** Asia **4** Central America and
the Caribbean **5** Africa **6** South America **7** Australia

Ethnic groups
2 Al**b**ania **5** Som**a**lia **3** I**n**dia **5** U**g**anda **2** Italy
4 Jamaica **2** Polan**d** **1** th**e** USA **3** Paki**s**tan
3 C**h**ina **4** Trinidad

The other Asian country is
Bangladesh

How's your maths?
1 Indian **2** Chinese / Bangladeshi **3** black Caribbean
4 Pakistani **5** black African

Slang
1 I'm just **chillin** with my **crew**.
2 What do you think of my **Tony Blairs**?
     They're really **phat**!
3 I love him. He's so **fit**.
     You're joking! I think he's **rare**.
4 Don't **diss** me!

pages 22 and 23
THE ASIAN INFLUENCE

True or false?
1 T **2** F **3** F **4** F **5** F **6** T **7** T **8** F **9** F **10** T

Asian words
1 curry **2** poppadom **3** bindi **4** bangle **5** joss sticks
6 kohl **7** chutney **8** pyjamas **9** bungalow **10** sari

The word 'curry' has been in English since the 16th century.

pages 24 and 25
FOOTBALL FUN

1 It's old!
2 We are the champions!
3 Sex symbol
4 It's popular!
5 Pub football
6 English rules!

The player is **Wayne Rooney**, the youngest footballer to
score for England.

pages 26 and 27
CRAZY ABOUT CRICKET

1g **2**c **3**a **4**b **5**f **6**d **7**e **8**h

Every two years they try to win
The Ashes.

Cricket rules
1 cricket bat **2** cricket ball **3** batsman **4** bowler
5 fielder **6** cricket pitch **7** wicket

Paul 100   Ray 90   Agnes 70   Julia 40   Bob 20

pages 28 and 29
RUGBY MANIA

A Very Short History of Rugby
There are FIFTEEN players in a team

1 helmet **2** gum shield **3** upper-body protection
4 rugby shirt **5** rugby ball **6** rugby shorts
7 socks **8** rugby boots

Class rugby match
  1 William Webb Ellis
  2 16
  3 Rugby Union and Rugby League
  4 15
  5 The shape makes it easier to carry.
  6 a scrum
  7 e.g. Australia, England, France, Italy, New Zealand,
     South Africa, Scotland, Ireland, Wales
  8 80 minutes
  9 Oggy, oggy, oggy …
 10 leather
 11 1979
 12 He always wears the same T-shirt under his
     English shirt

pages 30 and 31
THE 1950s AND 1960s

The Beatles changed pop music forever.
Teenage parents didn't like The Rolling Stones

a jewellery **b** skirt **c** sandals   **d** leather jacket
e jeans **f** motorbike **g** suit **h** scooter **i** jacket
j tie **k** trousers

Style
1950s Teddy Boys **4**   1960s Mods **3**
1960s Rockers **2**   1960s Hippies **1**

pages 32 and 33
THE 1970s AND 1980s

Glam rock	Punk
2 5	3 1 4

1c Mohican haircut P **2d** platform boots G
3e torn clothes P **4h** work boots P
5i safety pin P **6f** earring G/P
7g makeup G/P **8b** chains P
9a badge P

pages 34 and 35
THE 1990s TO TODAY

1 were liked **2** were created **3** were chosen
4 were written **5** were compared **6** was influenced
7 was watched

Style Wars
Goths (picture 1)
black
long black coats
white makeup black lipstick black fingernails
Marilyn Manson The Cure

Nu-Metallers (picture 4)
T-shirts of favourite bands
piercings in ears, lips, eyebrows
Limp Bizkit Blink 182

Grungers (picture 2)
trainers jeans with holes in them old T-shirts hooded
  sweatshirts
blonde dreadlocks
Nirvana Kurt Cobain

Gangstas (picture 5)
designer sportswear
jewellery
Eminem Destiny's Child

Pop Princesses (picture 3)
pink
silver jewellery
Will Young Gareth Gates Britney Spears

pages 36 and 37
THE SEASIDE

a surf board **b** wetsuit **c** flippers **d** snorkel **e** mask
f deck chair **g** seaweed **h** fishing net **i** mussel
j beach towel **k** crab **l** starfish **m** jellyfish
n shells **o** pebbles

Beach life!
a Cornwall **b** surfer **c** boring **d** trouble **e** beach
f clean **g** games **h** swimming **i** student

1E **2**D **3**B **4**A **5**C

pages 38 and 39
ON THE RIVER

1 ferry **2** canoe **3** yacht **4** barge **5** rowing boat
6 dinghy **7** power boat

1c **2**b **3**a

1 Oxford-Cambridge Boat Race **2** Great River race
3 Henley Royal Regatta

True or false?
1 F **2** T **3** F **4** T **5** F **6** F **7** T **8** T

pages 40 and 41
THE SEASIDE RESORT

1 Bournemouth **2** Blackpool **3** Newquay

Holiday confessions
1 camping **2** good **3** cloudy **4** tent **5** seals **6** trouble
7 Spain **8** holiday **9** sea **10** fell **11** sailing
12 tough **13** parascending **14** girlfriend

1 T **2** A **3** A **4** T **5** T **6** A

pages 42 and 43
WHAT'S ON THIS WEEK?

1 Zodiac The Red Lion
2 Oxygen The Riverside Leisure Centre
3 Hollywood Arena
4 The Riverside Leisure Centre The Red Lion
    Hollywood Arena Pizza City
5 Pizza City
6 The Riverside Leisure Centre
7 Nice Ice
8 Concept Dance Club Zodiac
9 Concept Dance Club

1 action **2** romantic **3** science fiction **4** historical
5 cartoon **6** horror **7** musical **8** comedy **9** detective

1 Can I have two tickets for the film on
    Screen 5, please?
2 Yes, of course. How old are you?
3 We're both thirteen.
4 OK, that's £10, please.
5 Here you are.
6 Thanks. Here are your tickets.
7 Thanks. Can we go in yet?
8 No, I'm afraid not. The doors open in ten minutes.

pages 44 and 45

PLACES TO GO

			1	f	r	o	g		
	2	c	a	r	a	v	a	n	
		3	p	i	r	a	t	e	
			4	r	u	g			
5	c	o	t	t	a	g	e		
		6	t	r	a	y			
		7	p	o	o	l			
		8	b	u	r	g	e	r	
	9	d	i	n	o	s	a	u	r
10	b	r	e	a	d				

The pub

1 Darts, billiards and dominoes are traditional pub games.
2 'Pub grub' is a slang term for pub food.
3 A 'Gastro pub' is a trendy pub serving high quality food.
4 Going for a pub lunch is a very popular British activity.
5 Only people over 18 can buy alcohol in a pub.
6 You can find Irish pubs all over the world.
7 Pubs often have live music.
8 Customers often stand up and sing a song in an Irish pub.
9 Pubs often have large screen TVs and show big football matches.
10 At 14 you can enter a pub but you can't buy a drink there.

Pub signs

1 The Crown 2 The Star 3 The Royal Oak
4 The Red Lion 5 The Bell 6 The Ship 7 The Swan
8 The White Horse

pages 46 and 47

MEETING UP

1 the park 2 the shopping centre 3 the youth club
4 the swimming pool 5 a fast food restaurant
6 the cinema 7 home

1 season ticket 2 bench 3 pop corn 4 cricket
5 sleep over 6 multiplex 7 skateboard park 8 pool

pages 48 and 49

CARNIVALS AND FETES

1 Where do you live?
2 What happens in the summer?
3 What do you like best at the fete?
4 What was the last fete like?
5 Did you buy anything?
6 What about the food?
7 Did you win anything?

1 Tombola 2 White Elephant stall 3 Cake competition
4 Throw the sponge 5 Egg and spoon race 6 Barbecue

Carnival time

1d 2c 3a 4g 5h 6b 7e 8f

1 Tropical Island 2 Ghosts 3 Pirates 4 Star Wars
5 Wild West

pages 50 and 51

MUSIC AND THEATRE FESTIVALS

1 Reading 2 Glastonbury, Edinburgh 3 Edinburgh
4 WOMAD 5 Edinburgh, Reading 6 Glastonbury
7 Reading 8 Glastonbury

[Insert completed word search from page 51]

1 Massive Attack 2 Robbie Williams 3 Motorhead
4 Atomic Kitten 5 David Bowie 6 Westlife
7 Coldplay 8 The Darkness 9 Radiohead
10 Fatboy Slim 11 Sugababes 12 Phil Collins
13 Pulp 14 So Solid Crew 15 Blue 16 Busted
17 Oasis 18 Iron Maiden 19 Ms Dynamite

pages 52 and 53

LET'S DANCE!

1 Morris dancing 2 Breakdancing 3 Salsa

1 breakdancing 2 morris dancing 3 morris dancing
4 breakdancing 5 salsa 6 morris dancing 7 salsa
8 breakdancing

Want to party? Why not go to a Ceilidh?

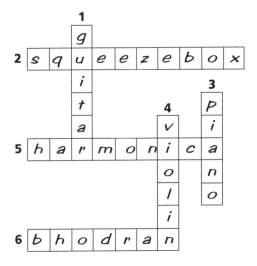

		1							
		g							
2	s	q	u	e	e	z	e	b	o	x
		i							
		t				4		3	
		a				v		P	
5	h	a	r	m	o	n	i	c	a
						o		n	
						l		o	
						i			
6	b	h	o	d	r	a	n		

pages 54 and 55

THE HIGH STREET

1 shirt 2 sweatshirt 3 belt 4 skirt 5 T-shirt 6 cap 7 coat
8 jacket 9 trousers 10 boots

Which shops is Janine calling from?
1 h **2** e **3** m **4** b **5** d **6** a **7** j **8** c

The shoe shop
I'd like to try on these trainers, please.
Of course. What size are you?
Size 7.
Just a moment. Here you are.
I'm afraid they're too small.
OK, would you like to try a bigger size?
Yes, these are much better, thanks.

The bookshop
Hi, I'd like to buy this book.
That'll be £5.99.
Here you are.
Thanks very much.
Would you like a bag?
No, thanks.

The chemist's
help
looking
This
much
It
have one
only

The newsagent's
Can I have a phone card, please?
Which card would you like?
A £10 one, please.
Here you are.
Thanks.

pages 56 and 57
TEEN SHOPPING

Gareth **2**   Will **10**   Kerry **9**   Martin **1**
Tamsin **4**   Anna **3**

Where would you go to ...
1 Top Shop **2** HMV **3** TK Max **4** The Gap **5** Lush
6 JD Sports **7** New Look **8** Borders

pages 58 and 59
BARGAIN-HUNTING

1 Sales **2** Charity shops **3** Car boot sales **4** Markets

pages 60 and 61
POCKET MONEY

a 6 **b** 4 **c** 3 **d** 1 **e** 2 **f** 5

Helping at home
Bryan gets £21.75 per week, so he has to save for 10 weeks
to buy an MP3 player that costs £200

1 Samirah **2** Iain **3** James **4** Richard **5** Iain **6** Lina

pages 62 and 63
PART TIME JOBS

[Label jobs for key? Here given as page layout]

1 Shelf stacker   **2** Cook
3 Paper boy   **4** Babysitter
5 Shop assistant

Where do these sentences come from?
a Babysitter   **b** Cook   **c** Shelf stacker
d Paper boy   **e** Shop assistant

Money management
1 Lucy **2** Ahmed **3** Ahmed **4** Chris **5** Melissa
6 Chris **7** Melissa **8** Lucy

pages 64 and 65
WORK EXPERIENCE

1 Bainbridge Publishing **2** photocopying, filing, checking
documents **3** very nice **4** yes

Things Max did wrong
He slept at his desk.
He arrived late three times.
He spilled cola over his keyboard.
He photocopied the wrong stuff.
He surfed the Internet.
He bought CDs online.
He was late with the photocopies.
He wrote his diary at work.

Jobs word search
1 architect **2** hairdresser **3** secretary **4** lawyer **5** engineer
6 journalist **7** police officer **8** chef **9** cleaner **10** waiter
11 actor **12** farmer **13** doctor **14** teacher **15** shop assistant

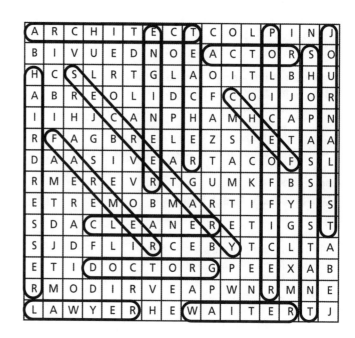

pages 66 and 67
SCHOOL RULES

1 running in the corridor.
2 having lunch out of school.
3 using a chat room.
4 using a mobile phone during a lesson.
5 wearing trainers.
6 listening to an iPod.

You must follow the rules
1 You must wear the school uniform.
2 You mustn't use your mobile phone.
3 You mustn't run in the corridor.
4 You must do your homework.
5 You mustn't listen to your iPod.
6 You mustn't chew gum.
7 You must arrive on time.
8 You mustn't smoke.

pages 68 and 69
SCHOOL SUBJECTS

Foreign Languages	English	Maths
Science	Biology	History
Geography	Art	Music
Physical Education	Drama	Computer Science

Jane
1 Art 2 Maths 3 Geography 4 Music
5 Physical Education 6 Computer Science

Monday Geography
Tuesday French
Wednesday Drama Computer Science
Thursday P.E. English
Friday Art Art

Mr Jamieson: Geography
Mr Allen: French
Ms Magrane: Maths
Mr Clarke: Drama
Mr Hall: Physical Education

pages 70 and 71
THE SCHOOL SYSTEM

Compulsory education
5 16
free education in state schools
private schools
Secondary school
8.45 3.15
maths
16 18
University
gap year
35% 40% 45%

Jimmy's diary
1a 2f 3h 4d 5g 6c 7b 8e

Who is …
Johnno is Jimmy's best friend. Ms Anderson is the English teacher, Alison is the girl Jimmy likes. Mr Blake is the headmaster. Mr Harrison is the science teacher. Jessica is Jimmy's sister.

pages 72 and 73
LUNCH TIME

1 Nick, Michael, Amanda, Dan, Alice **2** David, Stephanie, Lisa
3 Mary **4** David Stephanie **5** Alice **6** Lisa, Stephanie **7** Nick
8 David Lisa

Circles Sandwich Bar

1	2	3	4
2.90	2.50	2.30	2.80
1.90	2.50	2.20	1.50
1.90	2.20	2.20	2.20
___	___	___	___
6.70	7.20	6.70	6.50

Mike and Emily
1 have 2 I'd 3 Can 4 much 5 are

pages 74 and 75
BRITISH BREAKFASTS

1b 2d 3a 4h 5g 6i 7f 8e 9c

Porridge is made from oats.

Comfort food
1 F 2 T 3 T 4 F 5 T 6 F 7 T 8 F 9 T 10 T

pages 76 and 77
GLOBAL FOOD

Foods not mentioned:
duck snake kidney beans (although bean paste is mentioned) parsley oats

Pizza **Italy/the USA**
Chicken Tikka Massala **India/Britain**
Sweet and sour chicken **China**
Thai green curry **Thailand**
Chicken curry **India**
Nachos, tortillas, and tacos **Mexico**
Sushi **Japan**

Time for tea!
1 A 2 D 3 G 4 B 5 E 6 H 7 I 8 C 9 F

Pages 78 and 79
TYPES OF HOME

1 kettle 2 pets 3 microwave 4 shed 5 barbecue
6 garden 7 curtains 8 carpet 9 lawnmower

The other word in the word square is **computer**

Who lives in which home?
1 Jerry 2 Angela 3 Fatima 4 James 5 Ellie 6 Paul

pages 80 and 81
EXPLORE A BRITISH HOME!

Living room TV   coffee table   fireplace   armchair
computer (or in bedroom)
Kitchen microwave   fridge   washing machine
cupboards   dishwasher   kitchen table
Bathroom basin   toilet
Bedroom wardrobe   computer (or in living room)
Garden barbecue

1 watch 2 listen 3 eat 4 sit 5 isn't 6 have 7 called 8 has
9 use 10 spendn 11 love 12 playing

pages 82 and 83
BRITISH CUSTOMS

1 f **2** d **3** b **4** i **5** c **6** g **7** h **8** j **9** e **10** a

pages 84 and 85
CARDS, CARDS, CARDS!

a Miss you **b** Thank you **c** Love you **d** Get well soon
e Good luck! **f** Sorry! **g** Happy birthday **h** Congratulations

Choose the right card.
1 e **2** h **3** f **4** a **5** g **6** c **7** b **8** d

Special days
a 4 **b** 9 **c** 7 **d** 8 **e** 5 **f** 10

pages 86 and 87
SCHOOL PROMS

1 jewellery **2** flowers **3** prom king **4** prom queen
5 tuxedo **6** ball gown **7** crown **8** theme

already been to a school prom – Charlie Kevin Tracey
likes the idea of a school prom – Amanda Maxine

Prom night
1 a **2** d **3** f **4** e **5** g **6** c **7** b

pages 88 and 89
FIREWORKS IN BRITAIN

Fireworks code
Keep fireworks in a closed box.
Follow the instructions on each firework.
Light all fireworks at arm's length.
Stand well back.
Never go back to a firework after it has been lit.
Never put fireworks in your pocket.
Never throw fireworks.
Always light one sparkler at a time.
Never give sparklers to children under five.
Keep pets indoors.